Daring to Have
Real Conversations
in Business

Daring to Have Real Conversations in Business

by

JAMES PEAL

ZEMO TREVATHAN

TRISH BARRON

THOM DENNIS

Daring to Have Real Conversations in Business

James Peal
Zemo Trevathan
Trish Barron
Thom Dennis

Published by:
Leadership Development Group
2202 Damuth Street, Ste. 3
Oakland, CA 94602
510.336.0417
www.peal.com

Cover Design and Layout by gnibel.com

Copyright 2009 by James Peal, Ph.D.
ISBN, print ed. 978-0-9817748-0-0
First Printing 2009
Library of Congress Cataloging-in-Publication Data

James Peal, Ph.D., Daring to Have the Real Conversation in Business
1st ed 2009900333

TABLE OF CONTENTS

DEDICATION

To our ancestors, whose experiences in life have paved the way for our wisdom to grow, and to our children, who will carry them forward.

THE DARE

Ya know it doesn't matter what you call them: Heart-to-hearts, Face-to-face, Come to Jesus, Tough Love, Straight Talk, Walk-n-Talk, Fierce Conversation, Crucial Conversation, Moose on the table, Elephant in the room, Eat crow, Grab the bull by the horns, Tame the lion, Face the dragon, Face the music, Look in the mirror, Bite the bullet, The Brutal Truth, Get to the nitty-gritty, Cut to the chase, Speak the unspeakable, Tell it like it is, Tell the emperor, Open the kimono, Dress them down, Take 'em down a notch, Ego reduction, Reel 'em in, Confront the issues, Put a fire under their butt, Call them on their stuff, Burst their little bubble, Nip it in the bud, or Just blurt it out.

And it really doesn't matter what stops you from having these conversations: Whether there's a Lump in your throat, Knot in your stomach, Cold feet, Freeze up, Sucking up, Shut up, Cat's got your tongue?, Lips are sealed, Cone of silence, Gun to your head, Career-limiting move, "I'm confused," Beat around the bush, Sticking your neck out, Getting your head blown off, Head's on the block, Making an A of yourself, Covering your A, Getting your A chewed, Kissing A, Head up my...well, "Don't make a mountain out of a mole hill," "Don't be a tall poppy,"

"Mum's the word," "Not a peep out of me," "I'm not crazy," "I'm not a fool," "I'm not stupid," "I went blank," "If you don't have something positive to say, don't," Walking on eggshells? Being politically correct? Or maybe you're just fresh out of solutions.

No matter what you call them or why you won't have them...
the Real Conversations just won't go away...they're alive,
they bring you to life...
that's what makes them real...
Now since you are the leaders...
My question to you is...
whaddaya gonna do to bring the Real Conversations to life?
Because in this case...silence is NOT golden.

"The Dare" was inspired by Courtney Peal, a great (def-jam) poet. Jim Peal was moved to write this poem about Real Conversations — what we call them, why we don't have them, and why we need to have them.

PREFACE

*"Our lives begin to end the day we become silent
about things that matter."*
— *Martin Luther King, Jr.*

All of us are born into this world with the inherent ability to know and speak our truth. Sadly, most of us learn at an early age that we better not verbalize exactly what we are thinking or feeling. We receive various forms of negative reinforcement to not speak our minds. Everyone can remember your parents "shushing" you. Do you remember shushing your children? These habits are deeply embedded, and naturally, we practice and transmit what we have learned. Some of us received a sharp, disapproving look or loud criticism for telling it like it is; some of us were on the painful end of physical reinforcement (I received a spanking every now and then); and as we grew older, our schools and jobs reinforced the notion that we need to be very careful with our words. Yet paradoxically, telling the truth is the foundation of any strong relationship. This conundrum creates fear around being truthful.

At a systemic level in businesses, we have seen over and over how once the truth has finally been spoken, the whole system "sighs with relief" and then relaxes. The world turns more smoothly and peacefully in the frame of the truth.

Facilitating thousands of people of all ages and from all walks of life, we have had the opportunity to witness folks "coming to life," as they so often said. Even today, some fifteen or twenty years later, people tell us their lives were never the same again!

Telling the truth and having "Real Conversations" has transformed every facet of our lives. Each of us has experienced the high cost of avoiding Real Conversations both at work and at home. Relationships with family and friends are continually energized when we commit to having Real Conversations. Once we open up to share our truth with those we truly care about, we are consistently amazed.

From early on, Real Conversations have also been the key component in raising our children. Once the tough Real Conversations take place, it is remarkable how quickly a new space opens up for expressing and sharing connection, love, and humor.

We have spent much of our life helping ourselves and others unlearn much of our conditioning in order to return to our authentic selves. The results are profound. We can finally live productive and fulfilling lives nurtured with an inner satisfaction that can only come from being congruent and connected with our source. We believe that people are meant to be happy, and part of our happiness is based on being who we truly are and having the courage to share ourselves with others. One of the best ways to do this is to have Real Conversations.

— Jim, Thom, Trish, Zemo

> *"The truth is more important than the facts."*
> — **Frank Lloyd Wright**

ACKNOWLEDGMENTS

Special thanks go to those have taken our courses and have personally engaged in the material. Your willingness to tell your heartfelt stories, to share your personal quirks and vulnerabilities, as well as the unique things that make you tick, is inspiring. Thank you for the provocative and challenging questions, taking the tools to heart, and making positive changes in your life. Your insights, questions, and comments provide a rich and deep background that encourages and inspires. Thank you for passing your insights, knowledge, and wisdom to others.

It is a blessing to have great colleagues to work with and environments where we are able to freely bounce ideas off each other to create a business result. Acknowledgment goes to all the people who enriched our growth and development along the way.

Warmest regards go to our colleagues at GlaxoSmithKline (GSK) and especially Sherry Stuckey and Adrian Machon for their collaboration in the GSK Daring Conversations leadership program. We thank our colleagues at the Center for Professional Development, Charlotte Milliner and Simon Lovegrove. Much of the GSK Daring Conversations leadership program course was born out of collaborative discussions at the Center for Professional Development.

We also acknowledge Charlie Sheppard, friend and colleague for many years. Charlie is a world-class leader. His generous and creative spirit has consistently sourced leading-edge models for development and corporate leadership development programs. Many thanks go to the Cornerstone Executive Development Group, Stephen Xavier and Stacey LeBretton. Simon D'Arcy and Mark Brooks deserve special mention as they both in their unique way have woven their work, hilarious perspectives, and lives into ours. They both have helped us develop, teach, and model these basic practices of powerfully speaking our truths. Over the years our collaborative efforts with all of our numerous and valued colleagues have been for the purpose of serving our clients by bringing value around the world.

Deep thanks also to all of the courageous people we have worked with and learned from as clients over the past couple of decades. Their stories, challenges, and successes in generating Real Conversations are the lifeblood of this book. In fact, all of the dialogues in the book are inspired by or taken directly (and anonymously!) from our experiences with our clients, and we honor all of you for taking us up on The Dare and bringing your truths to your conversations.

This book would not have been possible if it were not for Ilene Segalove and Carolyn Hawkins, editors who have not only been instrumental in the production of this book, but have also helped our development on a professional level as well. Nancy and Neal get kudos for their love, support, and endless teasing and prodding to get Jim to finish the first edition.

Lastly, we acknowledge our children, Courtney, Sabrina, Alex, Sorrel, Ben, Leah, Lusi, and Rio, for inspiring us to do our best and be our best wherever we are.

Thank You!!!

"Be who you are and say what you feel, because those who mind don't matter and those who matter don't mind."
— Dr. Seuss

INTRODUCTION

*"The meeting of two personalities is like the contact
of two chemical substances: if there is any reaction,
both are transformed."*
— Carl Jung

It is impossible to fully engage in your life and not be changed by the work and the people that work with you. Real Conversations are the ones that make a difference. Throughout your day you engage in many different types of conversations. Some are the relationship building, "How are you doing today?", "How is the family?" type. Some conversations are the "I just bought the fifty-two-inch three-D TV and love it" or "Did you see that new Louis Vuitton?" kind. The type of conversations that we call "Real" are the ones that engage you fully in the game, create change, and move things forward.

Some people think that a Real Conversation is simply saying it like it is or confronting someone with what you don't like, but a Real Conversation is much more than that. Real Conversations can sometimes be challenging and so people often avoid them. By avoiding Real Conversations we put relationships at risk and often set ourselves up for making these conversations even harder than they need to be.

Most people tend to shy away from engaging in conversations that may be uncomfortable. You may think that you do not want to cause undue pain to others or yourself, but inside you know that much has gone unspoken. If you are like most people, ultimately, you want to operate from a deeper truth with more humanity and openness.

Do you tend toward one extreme or the other; "blunt" or "avoid"? Most of us go to both extremes but either we say nothing or we experience a major confrontation with sometimes disastrous consequences. Real Conversations involve saying ALL OF IT in a way that is completely CARING for the other person. This is why we love that Oscar Wilde quote so much: "The true genius of communication is to be totally honest and totally kind at the same time."

Silence is a sure killer of Real Conversations. Your job is to add value to the business. You have a unique set of talents, capabilities, and a unique perspective. Yet, if you remain silent, your value dissipates into the abyss. Why end your day with feelings of self-contempt or unfinished business when you can have Real Conversations and go home with a sense of deep satisfaction that comes from being fully engaged at work?

Real Conversations are powerful vehicles for engagement and transformation; they jump-start people into action and connection. All of us need a little jolt at one time or another to get things moving, and like jump-starting your car, Real Conversations require putting the right cables into just the right places. Have you noticed that kicking the tires and cursing a car with a dead battery will not get it running? Well, going into a meeting with a negative mindset, judgment, or false assumptions certainly does not get a conversation going anywhere either.

Having Real Conversations maximizes your effectiveness and the performance of your team. These conversations engage people and enhance accountability, creativity, alignment, and achievement. You optimize performance by telling people where they stand, what they are doing well and what they need to do to get back on course. Real Conversations create more freedom, more choices, more productivity, and they build a foundation of trust that is essential for high performance.

Leadership is about proactively engaging people. No matter the context or destination, an effective leader needs to know how to move beyond the status quo to turn the vision into results. Initiating the kind of conversations that are essential to engaging and inspiring your team moves you toward your goals.

Daring to Have Real Conversations in Business is about being fully alive, enthusiastic, and venturesome. This book will help you to gain important insights and knowledge about yourself that will really make a difference in all of your business endeavors. It takes you through the necessary preparation so you can start conversations, get the real issues into dialogue, and navigate your way to closure.

Daring to Have Real Conversations in Business is also about being strategic. Our purpose here is not to argue that "everything should be said" — that would be simply swinging to the other extreme. There are times and places where silence is appropriate. You must strategically choose the time and content of your conversations. This is different from keeping silent out of fear. Real Conversations start before we open our mouths, by taking an honest look at the situations and boundaries, connecting deeply with what we are committed to and to the commitments and intentions of the others around us, and then consciously choosing when and how to share our truths in service of those commitments and intentions. Sometimes our choice will be to best serve by maintaining silence. Our experience is that when these choices are made more consciously, not out of reaction to fears, everybody benefits.

You will read many examples of Real Conversations that took place and anecdotal examples from real-life situations that you can use to create your own approach. While the names and situations have been changed to protect confidentiality, every conversation in this book is a representation of Real Conversations that we have participated in or supported in our organizational and coaching work. Many of them are examples of situations in which people initially told us, "I just can't have a real conversation about that with him/her." But those who shifted their mindset and followed the principles were able to have successful outcomes.

Our intention is that you will find both inspiration and concrete suggestions in these examples of how you can overcome your concerns and obstacles for your own Real

Conversations. With practice, you will develop the tools and skills necessary to have Real Conversations as a matter of habit instead of the exception.

WHAT'S IN IT FOR YOU?

B eing aware of yourself carries the risk of being uncomfortable. As you embrace effective leadership, you choose a path that requires you to change and be changed by your situation and the people around you. Why bother? This is a tall order, yet leadership without this deep commitment will come across as inauthentic and shallow and your impact and results will be less than what they could be. Take on this task and you will reap the rewards of being a real person who engages in Real Conversations in your organization.

Positive intention is a primary key to having Real Conversations. This positive mindset creates a context that allows you to engage and learn from your experiences. The payoff is huge. Being conscious of who you are and what you are doing results in having quality relationships with everyone around you.

The process of creating positive intention requires awareness: specifically, being aware of your concerns, fears, and doubts; looking at the cost of hiding in your comfort or safety zone; and finally, learning how to use the tools necessary to step out of personal drama to become a true leader. In reality it may not be as black and white as the above statement might look. For some of you change happens around the subtleties and nuances of situations, your mindset, awareness, and actions. Without tackling the task of building self-awareness, leadership can become a series of calculated behaviors rather than an expression of your innate talents and strengths.

This book consists of three sections:

Part 1, What Is Real?
Part 2, Getting Real
Part 3, Being Real

What Is Real?

In the first section you'll get the essential components of a Real Conversation and understand the key Real Conversations that will make the biggest difference in your business. The purpose of this chapter is to set up the context so that you can understand what a Real Conversation is and the steps to get there.

Getting Real

This section is about developing your awareness, your mindsets, around the "Real" issues and situations and your communication skills. Part 1 focuses on the "what" regarding Real Conversations and Part 2 focuses on "how" you get there—the Real Conversation strategies. Much of a leader's development is about transforming your attitude or mindset, which is a much bigger task in many ways than knowing what to do. The "Best and Worst Practices" for Real Conversations are included in this section. The skills and tips include how to get yourself really present, how to navigate your own doubts and fears about having Real Conversations, how to connect with the other person, and what to say and what not to say to have an effective outcome.

Being Real

Part 3 consists of real-life stories that bring to life the concepts that are presented in this book, how somebody transforms their thinking and mindset from unreal to real, and the conversations that result. You'll see how you can turn unproductive conversations and meetings into valuable ones that move things forward.

When was the last time you had a Real Conversation? Not superficial chitchat. Not dumping. Not being political. We're talking about the kind of exchange that really matters, one that inspires and makes a difference. Each and every moment presents you with an opportunity to engage in Real Conversations. Once you experience their power and impact, you will never be able to or want to have just one! Rest assured, the people around you will join in, and in no time, you will have cultivated a culture of high performers who demand more Real Conversations. Grab hold, feel the juice, and open up your mouth; we dare you!

> *"Truth stands, even if there be no public support.*
> *It is self-sustained."*
> **— Mohandas Gandhi**

Part 1: What is Real

In the first section you'll get the essential components of a Real Conversation and understand the key Real Conversations that will make the biggest difference in your business. The purpose of this chapter is to set up the context so that you can understand what a Real Conversation is and the steps to get there.

Part 1: What Is Real

1. How "Real" Are Your Conversations?

2. The Top Three Real Conversations in Business

3. The Payoff and the Cost

"Two people in a conversation amount to four people talking. The four are what one person says, what he really wanted to say, what his listener heard, and what he thought he heard."
—William Jennings Bryant

THE INGREDIENTS FOR REAL CONVERSATIONS

In order for a conversation to be Real versus "UnReal," you need to have all of the following ingredients:

- You must be *fully present*. It is impossible to have a Real Conversation if your attention is on the clock, your BlackBerry, Blueberry, or whatever fruit is in your hand. To be real, it needs to feel personal and engaging. Your eyes, ears, mind, and heart need to be focused and open.

- There must be **truth-telling**. The meaning of "Real" is talking about what is really going on, both mentally and on a gut level. Be open and honest!

- A Real Conversation is a **two-way** street. It is not a drive-by attack, dumping on the other person, or a droning monologue. Asking questions, listening to answers, and mutual understanding is "Real" even if it makes you a little uncomfortable.

- Real Conversations are based in **positive intention** and create **trust**. This means that you go into the Real Conversation with the intention to create a positive result. You are willing to suspend negative thinking, be vulnerable, and take risks. Assuming positive intent means that you believe the other person has a positive intention whether it is evident or not, and despite your concerns, you are committed to giving them the benefit of the doubt.

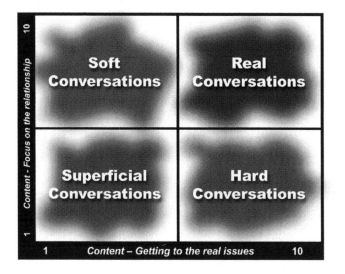

There are two types of Real of Conversations that you can have, Context and Content Real Conversations. The diagram illustrates a matrix where context, or the relationship, is on the vertical axis, and content, the real issues, are on the horizontal axis. The ideal situation is to rate a 10 on both context and content. When you are in the 10 zone, Real Conversations happen. The relationship is robust, there is a lot of trust and partnership, there is open communication, there is transparency, there is putting the real issues on the table, there is a two-way dialogue, and there is positive intent. That's a Real Conversation.

When you slide down the context or relationship axis, you get into superficial UnReal Conversations where there is little or no trust. You are being politically correct, there is skirting around the issues, and you really are going nowhere fast.

When you have a 10 on the context-relationship axis, and a 0 on the content-real issues axis, you are having a soft conversation. It's a friendly, feel-good experience, but you are not getting to the real issues. In this configuration, trust only goes as far as the good feeling goes, and consequently, when the warm fuzzies fade, the conversation ends.

A hard conversation is one that is filled with point and counter-point without any experience of trust or positive intent. These conversations are typically characterized by a sense of adversarial intimidation, manipulation, or pressure. Real issues are being discussed, but there is no real connection. Ultimately, this conversation is unpleasant and unsatisfying and usually ends with no desire to continue nor even to consider the possibility of a compelling future.

Context helps you build a safe space and encourages confidence instead of fear. Context Real Conversations are low risk because you do not have difficult content that you need to discuss. Instead, you can share all of your concerns, ask questions, and gather information. Once you get the hang of it, you'll find these relational conversations enhance your more challenging conversations down the line.

> *"Even if you are a minority of one, the truth is the truth."*
> **—Mohandas Gandhi**

"Change before you have to."
—Jack Welch

HOW REAL ARE YOUR CONVERSATIONS?

To jump-start the process of Real Conversations it's always nice to do an assessment in terms of your own conversations. Read the following real scenarios to stimulate your thinking about the types of opportunities for conversations at work. Then answer the following thirteen questions. The intention is for you to reflect on what you are thinking and feeling when you are communicating at work. The best way to go about this is just simply to answer with the first thing that comes to your mind. Don't try to outguess this particular assessment because it is just not that sophisticated.

REAL SCENARIOS

Notice what your thoughts and feelings are as you read about the following real-life scenarios from the field. You may have experienced some of them, or situations much like them. Others may take a bit of imagination, but make the effort to really put yourself into each scenario:

1. Feedback From Your Boss

Your boss has recently given you some feedback about your performance. He or she made references to negative perceptions that are "out there" about you but would not reveal the source of the perceptions nor when they were offered. In addition, he or she made general comments about the quality of your work but would not give you any specifics to improve. The meeting was concluded by your boss telling you that you need to fix the situation.

2. The Medium Performer

You are the manager of a team member who takes care of the basics, but not much more. Although he delivers on most objectives, you sense he is just not pulling his weight. You believe that he expects to be promoted in the near term and is generally unaware that his possible upward career progression is limited or indeed at a plateau. You need to clarify his performance (he's not as good as he thinks), manage his expectations, and find a compelling reason for him to improve.

3. High Performer With Issues

Your company has an effective manager with a strong reputation for getting results. Her team, however, finds her to be overly reactive and demanding when she is under pressure. She gets impatient and fails to listen, often cutting people off in mid-sentence. Her style creates an unpredictable atmosphere, and as a consequence, people avoid bringing issues to her attention. She often tells you about other organizations where people in positions comparable to hers get compensated at a higher level for the same job position. She wants to continue working for your company, but has a hard time rationalizing the pay difference.

4. The Difficult Personality Type

You are managing a cross-functional team to make process improvements across the business, including a member of the team who does not report directly to you. He is a good worker but has an extremely difficult personality. He likes to work on things individually and does not do well on a team. He thinks he is always right and does not listen to others. He is also very secretive about his work and doesn't want to share his knowledge with other team members because he wants to take all the glory. He rarely attends the meetings and when he does he is extremely argumentative. How do you deal with this personality and the issues that it causes with the rest of the team?

5. Organizational Change

You have been appointed to head a project to reorganize the customer interface in your business. Against a background of changing priorities, the project will undo most of the work from a previous project aimed at optimizing customer experience. Most of those involved in the previous project are still in the business. You are convinced the new project is the right way to go. To be successful, you need to get stakeholders in your business to buy into the idea. You are concerned about how to do this without making the previous strategy and its proponents wrong. You also need to make a convincing case to get the support you need from those at the sharp end who will have to make it work.

6. Thrown Under The Bus

One of the people on your team just returned from attending a meeting run by one of your peers. Your team member relays to you that your peer made some rude and condescending remarks made about your team's ability to perform and insinuated that your leadership was in question.

INSTRUCTIONS FOR THE QUESTIONS

Answer the following thirteen questions. If you wish, write the number of the question and your answer down in your notebook.

Answer these questions using one of the following sets of words:

1.   RARELY APPLIES
2.   OCCASIONALLY APPLIES
3.   FREQUENTLY APPLIES
4.   MOST OF THE TIME APPLIES

An evaluation section is provided at the end of the questions and includes specific chapter recommendations to help you make progress in areas where you need special assistance.

1.   ____There is a gap between what I am thinking and feeling about a business issue and what I say.

2.   ____ I often tolerate stressful or difficult situations at work that go on for a long time without addressing the issue.

3.   ____After having a critical discussion, I often think about what I should have said and may beat myself up over what I didn't say.

4.   ____ I have a hard time voicing my personal objections to business issues or people issues.

5. ____ I am concerned about retribution if I speak my mind at work.

6. ____ I avoid conversations that have an emotional charge or saying things that might upset others.

7. ____ I *do not* get quality, on-going feedback about how I am doing at work from my staff, peers, or boss.

8. ____ I *do not* offer my staff, peers, or boss feedback about how they are doing at work.

9. ____ People are often defensive when I give them feedback.

10. ____When anyone gives me feedback, I have a strong and sometimes negative reaction.

11. ____ I am unclear about my strengths and the areas I need to develop.

12. ____ I do not know how to start or work my way through a Real Conversation.

13. ____When taking a survey like this one, I tend to answer in ways that sound good or right rather than answering honestly.

_____ TOTAL SCORE

*"We spend our time searching for security
and hate it when we get it."*
—John Steinbeck

EVALUATION OF YOUR REAL ANSWERS

1. *There is a gap between what I am thinking and feeling about a business issue and what I say.*

It's normal to be cautious from time to time but if caution is the driving theme behind your behavior, you need to face your fears and learn how to have a Real Conversation. Caution often sounds like this: "I'm not really sure of the other person's intention. I'm worried about how she is going to take what I'm going to say." One of the very first Real Conversations to have with that person should be to address your cautions to set a context before you talk about the issues. What is it that has you a little unnerved? If this sounds too vulnerable, it is not. Truth-telling is the key to having a Real Conversation. Once you get the hang of it, you will find this conversation will inspire the other person to want to have more.

(Focus on: Part 2 Getting Real — Chapters 2 & 3)

2. *I often tolerate stressful or difficult situations at work that go on for a long time without addressing the issue.*

Given that you have to work in an environment with other people, tolerance is a virtue. However, if you find yourself tolerating too much, it may be that you have numbed yourself out and you are no longer aware of what is going on that needs to be addressed. This may manifest as consistent feelings of tension or exhaustion. Perhaps you assume it is futile to speak your concerns. This is a great opportunity to initiate a Real Conversation with a coach or mentor who can hear you and dialogue honestly. This Real Conversation will help sort through the issues and personal impacts, so you no longer have to take them personally. Then you are ready for the next Real Conversation with the person you actually need to talk to.

(Focus on: Part 2 Getting Real — Chapters 2 & 6)

3. ***After having a critical discussion, I often think about what I should have said and may beat myself up over what I did not say.***

We all get caught up in situations where we are not totally forthcoming. In these cases, our minds obsessively spin with the words we wished we had said. It can make us crazy! But blaming and beating ourselves up, a common phenomenon that happens when we are not getting to the real issue, will not stop the mind- loop from haunting us! Consider exactly what you were thinking that actually stopped you from putting the real issue or issues on the table. Why did you hold back? Was it a perception about the other person? Was it a perception about your own skills or inabilities? Did the issue have too much of an emotional charge? Uncover the root cause first, and then you can have a Real Conversation.

(Focus on: Part 2 Getting Real — Chapters 2, 3, 10)

4. *I have a hard time voicing my personal objections to business issues or people issues.*

It is important to be able to express your objections in a way that creates a positive impact. But if you find that your answer to this is "frequently," admit that you generally do not say what you are thinking. It really is your responsibility to get your ideas out on the table, especially when it comes to critical business decisions. Also, check to see if you are equally vocal on both the people and the business side of the equation. Some people are vocal when it comes to business issues, but when it comes to people, they clam up. If you are a leader and your point of view is assumed but not known, you may end up surrounded by a "yes culture." You may also give the impression that you do not want to hear bad news or objections, so everyone agrees with everything you say. Sometimes this can get you into trouble.

(Focus on: Part 2 Getting Real — Chapters 3, 10, Part 3 Being Real — Chapters 10, 11)

5. *I am concerned about retribution if I speak my mind at work.*

Most people have some concern about retribution. However, if this is the theme for you at work, introspection is called for. Consider communications with your leader about his or her feedback style and how to disagree. This will set up a safe context for speaking up at work. Learn to step up and be an active participant.

(Focus on: Part 2 Getting Real—Chapters 2, Part 3 Being Real—Chapters 10, 11)

6. *I avoid conversations that have an emotional charge or saying things that might upset others.*

It is important to understand how your personal history impacts you today. Depending on your family of origin, communication patterns, and the types of communication you are accustomed to in your business career, you may have strong feelings about not upsetting others. You may believe that telling the truth will damage or bring up hurtful emotions in people you care about, so you keep quiet at any cost. Keep in mind that if people do get upset, typically it is for a very short time. Quite often they will come around to see the truth in what you are saying and will recognize and appreciate your positive intentions. For potentially emotionally-charged conversations, you need to have a clear structure for working through the real issues.

(Focus on: Part 2 Getting Real—Chapters 2, 3, 10.5)

7. *I do not get quality, on-going feedback about how I am doing at work from my staff, peers, or boss.*

You are likely operating in what we call a "blind spot." The worst possible scenario is that you are a legend in your own mind. That is, you think you are doing great, but if we were to talk to the people you work with, they would have quite a different opinion. It is important to proactively ask for feedback. If people fail to give you the feedback you need, then it is up to you to ask yourself, "Why do I not get the feedback I want? What about my behavior keeps everyone so silent?"

(Focus on: Part 2 Getting Real: Chapters 5, 6, 7)

8. *I do not offer my staff, peers, or boss feedback about how they are doing at work.*

Most people will cover one base. Only extraordinary leaders cover all three. If you answered "never" or "seldom," it means you definitely need to ramp up your ability to give feedback. Once again, setting the context for Real Conversations and having a structure and format will help you be successful, not only in giving feedback, but in creating a culture of Real Conversations. A sample context-setting opener might sound like this: "If an issue arises, can we take a few minutes to talk about it directly and honestly with the intention that we are doing it to enhance our working relationship?" Once you have that fundamental agreement in place, it will set the stage for future feedback.

(Focus on: Part 2 Getting Real — Chapters 2, 5, 6, 7, Part 3 Being Real — Chapters 5, 6, 7, 10, 11)

9. *People are often defensive when I give them feedback.*

The response that you create in others is the measure of your communication. If you answered "frequently" or "always," it means that you probably hold some sort of negative intention about people when you give them feedback. If you are not aware of your mindset, do some introspection about how you feel toward people to whom you have given feedback and with whom you have met defensiveness. You will probably notice a limiting label glued to this person's forehead. In your mind's eye, you have already identified them as "needy," "greedy," "arrogant," or "lazy." This kind of preconception sets up a nonverbal context that the person responds to, often unknowingly. The first step in creating successful Real Conversations is to be aware of your perceptions and thoughts about the other person or group with whom you will be communicating. You need to shift operating from negative intention, which causes people to have a defensive reaction, to positive intention. Only then can you have a Real Conversation.

(Focus on: Part 2 Getting Real — Chapters 1, 6, 7,11, Part 3 Being Real — Chapters 5, 6, 7)

10. *When anyone gives me feedback, I have a strong and sometimes negative reaction.*

You may have thoughts like this: "I know for myself that I am not perfect, but I like to be damn near. So when somebody gives me what sounds like negative feedback, I do have a reaction. That is because I really care and want to do my very best." Sometimes just verbalizing your thoughts to others lets them know how much you value their feedback. Because you are dedicated to doing your best, receiving feedback that has a critical ring can initially feel hurtful. Pause and recognize that without an honest evaluation you may continue to miss the mark and ultimately your performance will suffer.

(Focus on: Part 2 Getting Real — Chapters 5)

11. *I am unclear about my strengths and areas I need to develop.*

So often we get feedback that's only positive or only negative. But everyone deserves a full and balanced picture of his or her performance. You do not want to focus just on the positives. You need to find out where your edge is. Where is the place you can develop and grow? Likewise, if you are always focused on your faults, you need to acknowledge your successes and focus on how you can leverage your strengths. How proactive are you in getting feedback from your boss and key stakeholders? It is a risk to ask, "How am I doing?" If you remain passive or in fear of asking that question, you may have to wait until performance review time, and by then, it may be too late to make course corrections.

(Focus on: Part 2 Getting Real — Chapters 5, 10, Part 3 Being Real — Chapters 3, 7, 10, 11)

12. *I do not know how to start or work my way through a Real Conversation.*

Having a format works. Often you can share the format as an agenda. This will help both you and the person with whom you are communicating manage your conversations to make them successful Real Conversations.

(Focus on: Part 2 Getting Real: Chapter 10)

13. BONUS QUESTION: When taking surveys like this one, I tend to answer in ways that sound good or right, rather than answering honestly.

This question is all about being politically correct. If you find yourself hesitating or thinking to yourself, "Well, if somebody else were to see this, it might be damaging," then it might be worthwhile to retake the entire survey and answer honestly. Rather than B.S.ing yourself, pause and then tell the truth. It's the only way you can even begin to have a Real Conversation. As your coaches, we suggest you read the book cover to cover!

You will gain more confidence in handling those situations at work that have been problematic as you read this book. You will also learn how to get to the real issues at hand instead of being hostage to them. Ultimately you will look forward to having meaningful Real Conversations that make a difference.

"When you are through changing, you are through."
—Bruce Barton

"Let your dreams outgrow the shoes of your expectations."
— Ryunosuke Satoro

THE TOP THREE REAL CONVERSATIONS IN BUSINESS

This book covers a lot of ground and focuses primarily on the most important Real Conversations you need to have with people at work. These are based on questions everyone asks, over and over again, in every job, no matter the person's gender, ethnicity, or position. Maybe you have addressed these questions in the past in one form or another or perhaps they are topics that slip by the wayside in the deluge of work you are managing. Making your conversations "Real" will change everything from the way you feel to the results you will definitely see. Real Conversations happen at the right time, not just in annual performance reviews. We will get into them more deeply in the body of the book, but here's a brief overview of the top three. The questions are:

1. **Direction:** Where are we going?

2. **Expectations & Feedback:** What is expected of me? How am I doing?

3. **Development:** What are my development opportunities?

1. Where are we going?

This question initiates a Real Conversation about your organization's direction and commitment. It asks: What direction are we going? What is the vision? How can we align and commit to the plan? This Real Conversation provides a context in which to share the vision as well as a place to engage people to openly commit and get on board. Posting your vision on the website is nice, but if you want it to come alive inside of people, then the vision must be communicated personally and in active dialogue.

2. What is expected of me? How am I doing?

"What is expected of me?" is a primary Real Conversation starter that creates the link between the goals of your organization and the performance of the employee. Everyone wants to know what the goals are so that they can be productive and create value for the business. Clear expectations and goals set the ground for productivity, process, and personal behavior. When leaders assume that people will just figure the answers out for themselves, it usually leads to frustration and confusion. While most people do not like to be micromanaged by being told how to do their job, they do need to know what the goals are.

"How am I doing?" This Real Conversation is based on a question that people are often afraid to ask of their peers, their subordinates, and especially their boss. They want to know if they are on track, but in many organizations people literally go years without any quality feedback. This Real Conversation provides a balanced look at the person's performance, not just the positives and not just the negatives. It promotes an honest look at the edge of their performance and welcomes ideas about how to improve.

3. What are my development opportunities?

No one wants to stagnate on the vine. Talking about my development opportunities is one of the most common Real Conversations people want to have. What are my developmental opportunities? How am I going to grow as a professional? How am I going to be promoted? When you have a Real Conversation with people about development you demonstrate your commitment to their growth. In addition to creating a place to brainstorm about what is possible, you are providing motivation to contribute and sustain their participation in your company.

According to statistics compiled by Career Innovations, approximately 40 percent of high performers in major organizations think about having Real Conversations with their managers and bosses but fail to do so. Why? Their answers vary from being habituated to not talking about real issues to recognizing that the leadership does not support a time or place for this kind of thing. Performance reviews do not really count because they are infrequent and are structured around a standardized document at a prescribed time.

The cost of not having these conversations is huge. Statistics tell us that these high performers are three times more likely to engage in planning to leave their job because they can not fill what is called "the conversation gap." It does not take a Ph.D. in calculus to recognize the cost of the intellectual horsepower that is being wasted while key people are planning their exit strategies rather than working to contribute to the organization. Real Conversations make a tangible difference!

"*Silence can generate feelings of humiliation, anger,
resentment that if go unexpressed contaminate every
interaction, shut down creativity and undermine productivity.*"
"Is Silence Killing Your Company?"
Harvard Business Review

WHAT IS THE PAYOFF
AND THE COST?

THE COST OF UNREAL
CONVERSATIONS

Leslie Perlow and Stephanie Williams in a *Harvard Business Review* article, "Is Silence Killing your Company?"
state that the social virtues of silence are reinforced by our

internal survival instincts. While some organizations say "speak up," leaders nonverbally communicate that falling into line and keeping quiet is the way to keep your job. Most people who go against their companies or express their concerns are punished either directly or indirectly by being marginalized and made to feel irrelevant. They go on to say that silence is not only ubiquitous and expected, it is also extremely costly to organizations. Silence usually starts when you choose not to express a difference. There is an enormous pressure to be part of the group and not to stand out.

THE ESSENCE OF CHOICE

Do you ever feel like you have two different characters sitting on your shoulders? There is Positive Intent on the right encouraging you to tell the truth, and there is Negative Intent on the left telling you to do anything but. You are unavoidably stuck in the middle certainly, with the free will to choose to whom to listen but often confused, numbed out, or worse.

When you choose Positive Intent, you will instantly risk something, but you also engage with the world. You will begin to cultivate self-acceptance and appreciation of others. Thinking and acting with positive intent creates a context of opening yourself up. Connection, compassion, and contact are possible. When you choose negative intention, you cut yourself off and see others through a lens of criticism, fear, and judgment. You literally shut down and find yourself inhabiting a world of false assumptions, worries, what ifs, and oh nos.

Positive Intent connects you. Negative Intent isolates you. Being in your head is not bad in and of itself; however, it is a problem when, because you are locked in your head, you pass up the opportunity to make a vital communication out of fear. Negative intention is certainly not the best place to begin if you want to create reasonable, compassionate, or growth-oriented conversations or decisions. It is crucial to learn how to come from positive instead of negative intention. Thinking and operating from positive intentions is the foundation for moving through your fears and doubts and entering into the kind of Real Conversations you want and need.

"It is not necessary to change. Survival is not mandatory."
— W. Edwards Deming

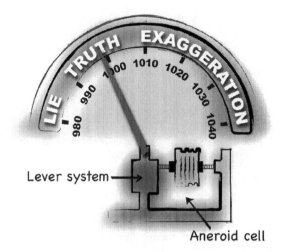

"If you tell the truth, you don't have to remember anything."
—Mark Twain

YOUR TRUTH BAROMETER

You always have the choice to speak or not speak the truth. If you are not speaking the truth, for the sake of simplicity, you are lying. Your body comes with a built-in barometer for knowing when it is telling the truth or not. That's right, you are actually built to know how the truth feels.

When you speak the truth, you feel an even, easy flow of energy, and when you hear the truth, it resonates inside of your body in an unencumbered way. When you lie, there is a distortion or fragmentation in that energetic, palpable flow. When you hear someone lie, you know it, maybe not in a verbal way, but something shifts inside of you. Yes, truth and lies express themselves as physical sensations that can be read and evaluated.

Think about a time someone told you an obvious lie or when you bent the truth out of shape. Remember how it felt? Do you feel tense thinking about it? Do you feel a sinking sensation in your gut? How about a surge of adrenaline or agitation or a kind of anxiety and panic? Your body actually responds to the memory of those kinds of disconnected, but uncomfortably familiar, sensations.

When you were a little child, it was natural for you to simply state whatever you were feeling or thinking. Kids usually blurt out the truth in an unedited fashion. But part of growing up in our culture is learning how to hold back our words, to couch them, to be polite, and eventually hide or avoid the truth. Children are told to bite their tongues and shut up or they are told that telling the truth is rude. These lessons get reinforced as you become an adult. With each job and relationship you continue to think that overt lying and telling white lies are ways to successfully function and survive. You may not call it lying; maybe you think you are being politically correct, sensible, or even prudent, but those euphemisms don't really work. No matter what you call it, it isn't the truth.

In order to have a Real Conversation, you need to unlearn some of the habits that you took on as you grew up. In order to change, you need to understand what you are doing right now. Do you lie? Or maybe, do you tell untruths? Do you rationalize this behavior by saying you need to protect someone else? What are your excuses? If you can admit that you do not always tell the truth, no matter the reason, you are well on your way to freedom, truly inspired leadership, and the ability to have powerful, compelling, productive Real Conversations!

Gary, a CEO, told his leaders, "To be on my team, you need to have your whole brain in the game. I expect each one of you to fully engage with the challenges at hand and to always come up with the best ideas possible. In order to do so, I need you to be direct and forthright in your communication with me and everyone else. No tiptoeing around on eggshells! You were hired because you have a unique set of talents, capabilities, and, most importantly, your own point of view. I expect you to be able to express your differences to fully leverage your intellectual capital. If you are not contributing fully, this business is not getting its full value for the money it is paying you and it's a waste of resources. Remember, other people will notice when you are not engaged and they often will follow your lead. Where does that take us?"

Does this sound like your organization? Is it a place where people feel free enough to discuss their opinions, even if they are controversial? Is it a place that supports conflict and encourages open resolution?

What Happens When Real Conversations Don't Happen?

Al, a divisional leader of research, was experiencing communication difficulties with his boss, Roger. "I disagree with a lot of what he says," Al confided to his coach. "I just think he's going down the wrong path. In many ways, he's totally ineffective, and I have to admit I don't like his style of leadership either."

The coach asked, "Well, have you said any of that directly to him? Have you had a Real Conversation?"

He responded, "No, of course not."

The coach probed a little deeper. "Al, what is stopping you?"

"I'm at a critical point right now. You see, my retirement is pending, and I need to have Roger write my final materials. I'm afraid if I bring up these issues prior to him finishing my review, he will certainly not approve my retirement bonus. I have been here for twenty years and I don't want to blow it now."

The coach said, "You know there is an incredible cost to your not speaking your mind, don't you?"

Al said, "I understand on one level, but the actual tangible financial cost concerns me more."

Not long after, Roger chose to release Al. Privately, he explained: "Al just sat there totally disengaged during our staff meetings. I could tell that he was seething inside, but he would not say what was on his mind, even when I tried. When I asked him direct questions, he totally avoided answering. I did not know what was going on with him, maybe some kind of weird hidden agenda, but I've got to be honest, I couldn't trust the guy anymore."

In this case, Al was attempting to play it safe by avoiding Real Conversation, and his strategy backfired. His decision to keep quiet actually sabotaged his future. He never grabbed the chance to speak his truth and left without his coveted retirement bonus. This particular case illustrates how not speaking out and harboring a hidden agenda can become a true liability that is detrimental to both the individual and the organization.

Step Outside Of Your Comfort Zone

Do the following exercise with another person acting as your coach. Then switch roles. Your coach's job is to ask you the following questions and simply witness your answers. The coach is not there to answer questions or come up with solutions. They are there to hold you accountable. Take your time thinking about and then responding to the questions. Don't rush. The process can take as little as ten minutes or up to an hour. It is often helpful to write notes to yourself as you respond. This exercise gives you a chance to step out of your comfort zone and allows you to honestly observe habitual patterns that have limited you from engaging in Real Conversations.

1. Does your boss have Real Conversations with you?

2. Do your peers have Real Conversations with you?

3. Does your staff have Real Conversations with you?

    • How do you know?

    • What stops you from taking a leadership role in those conversations?

- What stops you from asking for honest feedback?

- What is the risk for you personally?

- How do you verbally and nonverbally send signals that it is not OK to approach you?

- What is your preferred way to receive feedback?

- What are your hot buttons/charged subjects around feedback?

- How will you communicate your feedback preferences to those with whom you work?

4. What does it cost you/your organization when you avoid these topics?

- Energy level

- Performance and productivity

- Attitude and morale

- Self-concept

- Health

- Carryover to other relationships (friends, primary relationship)

5. What actions are you now going to take?

More than likely you have a set of convincing reasons why you should not speak up and engage in the Real Conversations. No matter your rationale, you want to play it safe. Yes, fear still runs you. It is no surprise that individuals or organizations that play it safe rarely win the game. Ask yourself, "How can I win from the sidelines?"

Take a serious look at the cost of promoting silence in your organization. Productivity and personal satisfaction suffer when people are not engaged. The loud silence you may hear speaks volumes about how energy and brainpower are being thwarted or even destroyed.

When you have something crucial to say and you withhold it, you create stress. This type of stress is self-manufactured, but nonetheless, it takes its toll. There are three main ways this kind of tension affects you personally: physically, mentally, and emotionally.

What happens to you physically when you have something to say and you do not say it? The only way that you can really withhold communication is to create tension in your body. Where in your body do you hold tension? It takes energy to hold back from what you are thinking and that shows up physically because your muscles are being held tight. You will feel drained at the end of the day because you were working hard to hold your muscles tight and your mouth closed! When your physiological system goes into fear mode, your body secretes excess amounts of substances that prepare you for flight or fight. This type of stress can lead to ulcers, other digestive disorders, allergies, and rashes. Even arthritis or other inflammatory diseases can be exacerbated by chronic stress and tension. Perhaps you hold tension in your throat, shoulders, chest, or gut. Your circulation becomes constricted, and so do you. How can this response be beneficial?

What happens to your mental focus when you withhold communicating? Rather than focusing on the issue at hand and allowing ideas to flow into you, you are on guard. You know what it is like to be in the presence of someone who is on guard; it is draining.

You may beat yourself up because you are not weighing in. You end up victimizing yourself in a loop of self-talk that is critical and undermining. "Boy, what a wimp. I just couldn't open my mouth." "It would serve me right not to get promoted. I'm not worth it." "There goes another time you didn't step up. Now you will never recover." When you have that type of internal negative self-talk going on, your self-esteem naturally drops and you begin to lose confidence. The resulting doubt is crippling. This is a great cost not only to your professional life and the organization, but you may find your home life affected as well.

It is crucial to recognize and catch yourself as early as possible when you are feeling conflicted about speaking your mind. You'll know when the veil of fear and doubt descends and gets its grip on your body. You will also know what to do. You have been practicing breathing, becoming familiar with your fear, embracing it as a doorway into a Real Conversation, and now you can use the tools from this chapter to help you become even more honest. The more you add up the financial, physical, mental, and emotional cost of beating around the bush, the more you will want to stop, get a grip, and make truth telling and creating a two-way street for communication part of your repertoire.

CONSIDER THIS:

1. What does it cost you when you avoid having Real Conversations? Consider the emotional and financial costs.

2. What will motivate you to take action and have Real Conversations instead of avoiding them?

3. Choose one Real Conversation you want to have. How will you prepare? When will you have it?

"Exaggeration is truth that has lost its temper."
— Khalil Gibran

"The truth will set you free, but first it will make you miserable."
James A. Garfield

Part 2: Getting Real

This section is about developing your awareness, your mindsets, around the "Real" issues and situations and your communication skills. Part 1 focuses on the "what" regarding Real Conversations and Part 2 focuses on "how" you get there—the Real Conversation strategies. Much of a leader's development is about transforming your attitude or mindset, which is a much bigger task in many ways than knowing what to do. The "Best and Worst Practices" for Real Conversations are included in this section. The skills and tips include how to get yourself really present, how to navigate your own doubts and fears about having Real Conversations, how to connect with the other person, and what to say and what not to say to have an effective outcome.

Part 2: Getting Real

1. Check Your Attitude
2. Getting Through Fear
3. 5 Excuses Not to Have Real Conversations
4. To "Tell" the Truth?
5. Shrinking Your Blind Spot — Request Feedback
6. Growing Rapport and Trust
7. The Conversation Cycle
8. The Power of Silence
9. Dealing with Gossip
10. Best Practices for Real Conversations
    a. Have your opening line ready
    b. Frame and state the issues
    c. Be fully accountable
    d. Set the table at the beginning
    e. Hang in with emotions
    f. Cultivate emotional vigor
    g. Establish a plan
    h. Close with acknowledgment and appreciation
    i. Play a couple of scenarios in your mind
11. Worst Practices for Real Conversations
    1. Don't show up
    2. Avoid emotional content
    3. Blame and be defensive
    4. Be distracted, interrupt, and don't listen
    5. Be vague

Attitude!

"We convince by our presence."
— **Walt Whitman**

CHECK YOUR ATTITUDE

(From the book *Check Your Attitude at the Door*)

Your attitude speaks volumes before you utter a word. Your attitude sets the tone for how people respond to you. Most people do not realize that they are always communicating what they are thinking. Like your shadow, you often are unaware of it. You know immediately when someone has a "bad attitude" because of the toxic environment it creates; you feel it. Some people are a fight waiting to happen, or you may have seen the sign on someone that says, "Kick Me."

Your mindset is a collection of decisions that you have made about a person or situation that determine how you think and feel. Your attitude is how your mindset gets expressed. Your attitude permeates everything about you: the tone of your voice, what words you choose, what you say, and what is in between the lines. Your attitude determines how you move your body—your body language. Right now, take a moment to think about someone you like very much, and then notice how you feel. If you do not have a mirror handy, imagine what you look like right now. You appear relaxed. More than likely, you are smiling. Now think about someone you dislike and notice how you feel. Track your body sensations. Again, imagine what you look like from the outside. Did your mouth clamp down, your gut tighten up, or your pulse pick up speed? Now, take what you just observed and imagine how another person whom you dislike sees your nonverbals (your facial expression and body posture) when you are having a conversation with them. What about the tone of your voice when you speak to someone you do not like? Is it curt? Is it whiny? Consider having a conversation with another person coming from this place of negativity. How real can it be? How would you feel if someone approached you in this negative way? It certainly contaminates the potential of any good or productive results, and that is even before you get a word in edgewise!

While you may think that your thoughts and feelings are purely private, your body is mirroring and in fact is speaking your mind. What you are thinking and feeling gets translated into your body language and is very much like those electronic signs with a message that flashes, this time across your forehead. Dozens of nonverbal expressions and behaviors, from the furrow in your brow to the tension in your jaw to the angle of your gaze, silently broadcast your thoughts and feelings loud and clear.

Your body language actually has a larger impact on others than the words you speak. Although you may think words are the primary way you create impact, research done by Mehrabian (Mehrabian, Albert (1971) *Silent Messages* (1st ed.)) points out that people are largely influenced by your body language (as much as 55 percent of the impact) and your vocal qualities such as tone, volume, speed, and inflection of your voice (as much as 38 percent) when emotions are involved.

These factors come into play when developing trust. If your words do not match your body language and vocal qualities the receiver will perceive this incongruence and tend to unconsciously believe the message being communicated by the body language over the words. For example if you say, "Nothing is wrong" and you teeth are clenched and your shoulders are rigid, the receiver is going to believe the message that you are mad even though your words say that everything is fine. Since your mindsets and attitudes make up a huge part of having a Real Conversation, it is important to become aware of how you communicate nonverbally.

*"In a controversy the instant we feel anger
we have already ceased striving for the truth,
and have begun striving for ourselves."*
—Buddha

YOUR MINDSET

As we mentioned previously, whether you think you are an open book or not, you express yourself through an elaborate system of body postures, gestures, and poses. Your body is expressing or speaking what your mind is sensing or thinking. You may not know what signals you are sending, but others can read your nonverbal messages and get a lot of information about what's going on just by observing you.

Here is a story that explains how your thoughts are translated into body language:

Imagine for a moment that you are a bank teller. It's been a pretty good day but you look up and here comes someone in a bad mood. You already know he's not a happy camper. His head is hanging down. He is scowling. He walks with heavy steps and then stops at your window with his hands on his hips. He hands you a check to deposit and then pounds on your counter, points his finger at you, and raises his voice. In only a few moments you mumble to yourself, "This guy is a real jerk." After he completes his tantrum, you make the transaction and then he turns and storms out of the bank. Although this guy is gone the experience remains. The whole scene circles around and around in your head and you hear yourself repeat, "I can't believe what a jerk that person was!" until you are really bent out of shape.

At this point you feel the need for some sympathy so you lean over to the teller next to you. "Could you believe what a jerk that person was?" you whisper.

And she says, "Yeah." And so it is said, "Where two or more agree, then it must be true."

A couple of weeks go by. There you are at your window on another good day, and guess who walks in the door? And what do you suppose is the first thought that goes across your mind? That is right, "There is that jerk." You make a decision. "I am going to armor up, just in case that jerk comes to my window." And sure enough, the person comes to your window. Then you decide, "I am not going to take this crap." You prepare for a fight, hold yourself upright and stiff, and quietly put on your nonverbal boxing gloves. Today, however, that person is in a fine mood. When he walks up to the window he almost smiles, but then senses you are uneasy. He notices your scowl and crossed arms and thinks, "This teller looks like she wants to pick a fight. I better be ready for it." Then he becomes defensive and rude. And when the transaction is done, you say to yourself, "What an uptight guy. I was right. He is a real jerk." You don't realize that it was your nonverbal signals that set up his reaction.

If you have a negative mindset about the other person before you begin talking, what can you expect out of the interaction? This person is unconsciously reading your nonverbal signals and responding to them. Who is setting up whom? Who is being the "jerk"? Whose nonverbal signals are being seen and misinterpreted? Is there any chance of having a positive interaction?

This story illustrates how your thoughts, mindsets, are transformed into your body language and behaviors that can set up the reactions of other people. Now think about someone you have a hard time with. What are some of the negative thoughts or mindsets you have about them? Now step outside yourself and look at yourself through their eyes. What nonverbal expressions do they identify in you? Is your jaw clenched, are your shoulders tight, eyes narrowed? Is the tone of your voice implying, "You idiot" at the beginning or end of each sentence?

Most of the time you are not aware of the nonverbal signals that you are sending out, yet when you see how people respond to you, you might think it is all about them. What attitude have you conveyed without saying a word?

> *"Faith is taking the first step even*
> *when you don't see the whole staircase."*
> **— Martin Luther King, Jr.**

BENEFIT OF YOUR DOUBT

Another thing that gets you stuck is when you fall into a negative mindset. You assume the other person doesn't really care, doesn't really want to work, or is arrogant or lazy. When you assume negative intention you are thinking that your employee, colleague, or boss goes home at night and spends her time thinking about how she is going to ruin your day. It's as if she is saying to herself, "How can I make that person miserable?" or "How can I really do substandard work and get reprimanded?" Maybe that is a tad extreme, but certainly you may hold a strong judgment about the people with whom you need to talk. Negative assumptions and labels easily pile up, and it is next to impossible to enter into a conversation and be heard accurately because of all of the unexpressed thinking and assumptions that pollute the air. Bringing negativity into a room is no secret, and it generally provokes others to shut down, lash out, or worse.

When you realize how limiting it is to think in a negative way, it is finally possible to move forward and practice positive intent. Assuming positive intention allows you to give others the benefit of the doubt. This means you suspend your thinking about how right you are and how wrong they are. When you take a break from that kind of habitual, judgmental way of thinking, you create the possibility for something positive to happen. You are ready for a Real Conversation.

Let's look at how some behaviors can be reframed by positive intent. Assuming positive intent is the best way to break out of your own pattern of being negative.

Behaviors seen through negative intent	Behaviors seen through positive intent
Micromanaging	Attention to detail
Not a team player	Individual contributor
Impatient	Sense of urgency
Angry	Committed
Stubborn	Determined
Insensitive	Internally focused

As you begin to reframe your negative intentions into positive intentions, you will release the negative thoughts/mindsets you have about others. This creates the possibility for a positive exchange to take place. Assuming positive intention is a mindset that helps you become more comfortable at telling the truth, facing your fears, and moving forward.

Real Conversations happen when you are present. One behavior that keeps you out of the present moment is getting stuck in negative thought-pattern mindset. Focused introspection gives you the chance to interrupt and replace the mindsets that tend to sabotage your interactions with others. This chapter helps you understand how to honestly evaluate how you behave so that you can consciously shift from negative to positive intent. It teaches you how to use the model of Negative Intention and Positive Intention so that you can develop the powerful ability to choose how you want to be instead of living by default. Let's look at how thoughts, mindsets, and attitudes set the context for interactions in a day in the life of a bank teller.

"Your present circumstances don't determine where you can go;
they merely determine where you start."
— Nido Qubein

YOUR INTENTION

Your intention refers to your specific purpose or desired goal. Intention is what motivates your actions. Your intention is independent of whether or not the action will produce a successful or unsuccessful impact. Impact is what other people experience as a result of your behavior and/or actions.

You can understand more about the relationship between intention and impact by examining the following illustration. Four quadrants define how your intention and impact interface with one another to cause different effects. Depending on what your intention is and the impact that you have, your behavior will fall into one of these four quadrants.

- If you have Positive Intention and a positive impact, it is called authentic behavior.

- If you have Positive Intentions for others in a situation and have a negative impact, that is called missing the mark. Your intention is good; however, your behaviors don't create the impact that you desire.

- If you have Negative Intention and create a positive impact, this is labeled manipulation. Basically, you fool people into believing you, but you actually have a hidden agenda for your exclusive gain.

- If you have negative impact and Negative Intention, this is sabotage. Sabotage may be overt or covert, but typically it is covert. In other words, the other person doesn't have an awareness of what your intentions are, yet you are able to have a negative impact on them.

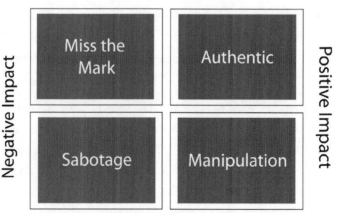

Most of the time when you operate from Positive Intention your motives are either overt (made clear) or there is transparency to them. You will either tell the other person up front what your intention is, or you will answer honestly when asked. There is nothing hidden. When people operate from Negative Intention they typically keep their motives covert (hidden). When somebody tries to make you feel good or does something positive just to take advantage of you, they usually will not tell you their intention. Likewise, when somebody says or does something to ruin you, they usually will keep their intention a secret.

Sabotage Scenario:

Frank had a negative perception of his boss and felt that she was selfish and out for her own good. Consequently, on several occasions when topics would come up in meetings, Frank chose to keep information to himself rather than share with the group and his boss. Consequently, his boss had a great deal of difficulty dealing with situations that came up because she did not know everything she needed to know. This resulted in her consistent failure at solving the problems at hand. This is a good example of sabotage. Frank had a Negative Intention and a negative impact.

Missing the Mark:

Roger wanted his team to work well together. When issues came up in staff meetings he would look at the person in charge and say, "Fix it." Sadly, this strategy did not work because more discussions needed to happen to move things forward. In this case, although Roger's intention was to empower the person to take care of the problem, it really didn't fulfill its purpose. His team needed him to interact further in problem solving. Roger had a good intention and thought he was empowering his team, but his communication had a negative impact.

Manipulation:

Steve felt that he always had to get people to do what he wanted. In meetings he would tend to have an overbearing way of steering the conversation toward his outcomes. He believed that the team wasn't quite capable of coming up with the right decision. After a meeting his team usually felt they had wasted their time because Steve had already decided the result and generally disregarded any feedback. His use of manipulative tactics created frustration. "Why didn't he just tell us what he wanted rather than pretend he wanted our input?" they would comment. The consensus was that Steve had a hidden agenda.

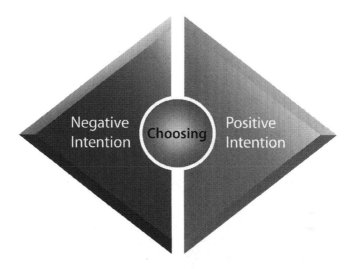

CHOOSING POSITIVE INTENTION

"There is little difference in people, but that little difference makes a big difference. The little difference is attitude. The big difference is whether it is positive or negative."
— W. Clement Stone

When you choose Positive Intention you instantly engage with the world. Your mind becomes open and more permeable, which gives you more access to the people around you. Self-acceptance and appreciation of others become your foundation. When problems arise you look toward a solution and take action versus blame and condemnation. Connection, compassion, and contact are possible. When you come from Positive Intention you speak the truth and you feel an even, easy flow of energy.

When you choose Negative Intention you cut yourself off and see others through your lens of criticism and judgment. Your mind hardens and little touches you because you are on the attack or are being defensive. Negative Intention creates the hard shell and all you can see are your own negative assumptions. You literally shut down and find yourself inhabiting a world of false assumptions, worries, what ifs, and oh no's.

Positive Intention connects you. Negative Intention isolates you, and out of fear you pass up the opportunity to make vital communications. Negative Intention is certainly not the place to come from if you want to make growth-oriented decisions or create Real Conversations.

It is crucial to learn how to come from Positive instead of Negative Intention. Thinking and operating from Positive Intention is the foundation for moving through your doubts and fears and allows you to enter into the kind of attitude that serves everyone. While it all starts with your thoughts, it all ends up in your actions.

Getting To Positive Intention:

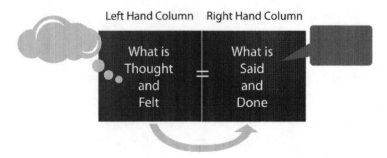

What Is In Your Left-Hand Column?

Peter Senge, an author on personal mastery in business, created a useful model called the Left-Hand Column, which helps you understand more about building a positive attitude. Here's how it works. Think of a recent important interaction that you had. Now draw a line down the middle of a piece of paper, creating two equal-sized columns. Under the left-hand column, list all of the things that you thought, felt, and wanted to say in your conversation, but did not. In the right column, list what you actually said. Finally, ask yourself, "How do the two columns compare? Is there a significant discrepancy?"

Look at the example below:

Tom's Left-Hand Column	Tom's Right-Hand Column
There is no way we can ever achieve that. How ridiculous. You are an idiot!	"Hmm, you bring up an interesting point."

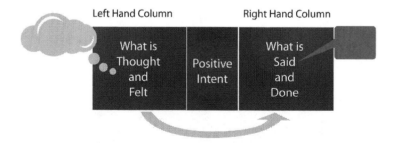

As you consider what is missing, you are actually building awareness of how to create more positive intent. Operating from Positive Intention is about achieving some sort of equality between what is in your left-hand column — what you think and feel — and what is in your right-hand column — what you actually say. Obviously, you aren't going to utter every thought in your mind, but in order to have a meaningful interaction you need to make sure you express what is important during your actual exchange. The next chart illustrates the addition of a Positive Intent column to show how you can transform your thinking into speaking, and a new right-hand column to show how the communication changed.

Tom's Left-Hand Column	Positive Intent	Tom's New Right-Hand Column
There is no way we can ever do that. How ridiculous. You are an idiot!	This person is thinking outside the box. They are being very creative. They want to stimulate discussion.	"Help me connect the dots here. I am not sure how you arrived at your solution. What was your thinking? How did you come up with that solution?"

"Do you know the difference between education and experience? Education is when you read the fine print; experience is what you get when you don't."
— Pete Seeger

"I don't like that man. I must get to know him better."
—Abraham Lincoln

RAISE THE FLAG EVERY DAY

L iving Positive Intention has been described as raising a flag every day, but there is no place to tie it. Practicing Positive Intention requires intention, attention, and expectation. As you commit to operating from Positive Intention, expect that you will be given many opportunities and be repeatedly challenged to maintain that positive attitude. As long as you can expect to be challenged, you can use the challenge, embrace it, and learn more about yourself and increase your mastery. Positive Intention is not a destination; it is an evolutionary spiral that enhances life. Again, you will have infinite opportunities to Check Your Attitude and change your thinking and actions. Grab them and practice raising the flag.

As with athletic training, you might feel a little sore when you begin, but with practice you will gain a level of expertise and actually create the experience of Positive Intention for yourself and for others as well.

GUT CHECK

Your first response to challenging events and situations is one gauge to measure your progress and level of mastery. How do you feel? Be as aware of your thoughts and feelings as possible. When you build this level of vigilance from a non-judgmental place it will help you make great leaps. Simply notice your mind, thoughts, and feelings without knee-jerking yourself into a reaction. This pause and attention will build your ability to make Positive Intentional choices about your life. Check Your Attitude and become an active observer of your mind. It will instantly help to neutralize negative reactions.

PRACTICE 3 STEPS TOWARD POSITIVE INTENT

1. Acknowledge your first thought.

2. Suspend Negative Intention and seek Positive Intention.

3. Frame your situation and formulate a good question that you can ask the other person to engage him or her in dialogue.

Jamie has a way of bragging about herself. She often talks about her role in things and what she accomplished to the exclusion of promoting other people or people around her. Every time Tim would hear her front-page herself he would cringe and regret his association. In this situation Tim decided to pause for a moment and ask himself, "What is she trying to do by promoting herself?" After some thought he realized that she needed to be acknowledged and that she was doing it for herself because she did not hear it from the outside. Two things happened for Tim after he had that realization. One was when he heard her acknowledging and boasting about herself he had a neutral reaction, and from time to time he would actually compliment her on the work that she did. In this situation Tim changed from wanting to be right about how wrong she was for self-promotion to understanding her situation and actually contributing to a solution. Everyone likes to be acknowledged anyway.

This practice works to transform how you approach difficult situations. It may seem awkward at first, and it may feel like it's not the right thing to do. This sensation is resistance. When you assume Negative Intention, your mind wants to be right about how wrong others are. This is an effective time to push the pause button on your negative thinking so that you can create the possibility for a positive result to occur.

Your mind has been conditioned to be right at the expense of making others wrong. Often you may think, "Well, that person is wrong and I am obviously right." Even if you are right, a problem develops when you need to point out that she is wrong and insist that you are right. This one-upmanship creates a hostile environment. To shift the interaction to the possibility of having Positive Intention you need to ask yourself, "How do I lead her to this result or conclusion in a way that she is going to feel OK?"

You will have to practice assuming positive intent over and over until it becomes a natural way of thinking and acting. Do not expect it to happen automatically, but in time you will easily shift your thinking, and you will be amazed at the results as you find yourself engaged in potent dialogues and interactions that change and improve everything you say and do.

Emotions have a Positive Intention. Look at the chart below to get a sense of what the Positive Intention could be for disappointment, anger, and stubbornness. In addition to the Positive Intention there is a column giving a few tips on how you might approach someone in that emotional state.

Emotion	Emotion — Process	Positive Intent	Engage them by...
Disappointment	Is let down by an expectation that is unfulfilled.	Has high expectations and is committed to results.	Acknowledge the goal he/she wants to accomplish. Reassure in your confidence in his ability to achieve.
Anger	Something is not going as expected. A defense for the fear of losing something, or failing.	The person knows what they want. Has a lot of energy and focus. Has a sense of urgency.	Convey your understanding of his/her goal. Ask about the concerns and what steps can be taken to mitigate.
Stubbornness	Resistant to change.	The person wants to be certain that results can be achieved in a new direction.	Ask for what criteria need to be fulfilled in order to shift. Ask about concerns.

NEGATIVE INTENTION

When you are coming from Negative Intention you shut down and your awareness turns into a thick shell that constricts you. You only see and hear your own thoughts and feelings. When you are in Negative Intention you are convinced that you are right about what you perceive and feel. You abdicate responsibility for your life and begin to project negative qualities on yourself, others, and the world. When you operate from Negative Intention your world also seems like it is filled with people who are negative. You put a negative spin on the events in your life as well as on what people say or do.

You will be way ahead of the game if you can honestly identify how you play the roles in the Negative Intent Molecule as you interact with people. If you deny that you ever operate from this place, you are fooling yourself. Face it, everyone has nonproductive personality traits, and the sooner you admit it, the easier it will be to create other, more useful, choices.

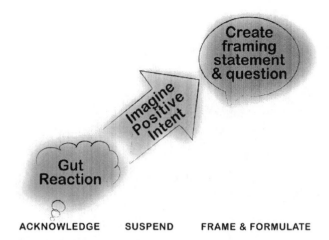

ACKNOWLEDGE   SUSPEND   FRAME & FORMULATE

PRACTICE POSITIVE INTENT: ACKNOWLEDGE, SUSPEND, FRAME & FORMULATE

1. Acknowledge your first thought.

2. Suspend negative intent and seek positive intent.

3. Frame your situation and formulate a good question that you can ask the person to engage him or her in dialogue.

It is a three-step process to transform your thinking from negative intent to positive intent. Let us look at how the process applies to the previous section. When you have a negative reaction:

1. Notice and acknowledge your first gut reaction, your first thought. This is what is unspoken and shows up in your left-hand column. What is unspoken speaks volumes and gives you a lot of valuable information that will lead toward deeper self-awareness. First thoughts are often negative and may eliminate solutions in one fell swoop. "There is no way we can ever achieve that" cuts out possibilities. They often make the other person wrong as in, "That is ridiculous." Also, once you label and make judgments about the other person, you actually stop relating to him and instead you get stuck on your own private assessments. Since your thoughts control your nonverbal signals, how do you suppose the other person is being impacted by your nonverbal messages? If you read your left-hand column and identify that you are operating in a negative loop, the next step is to...

2. Suspend your negative thoughts for a moment and instead ask yourself, "What is this person's positive intent? What are they trying to accomplish for the greater good?" Consider: "This person is thinking outside the box." "What is the value he is trying to bring to the company?" "He is being very creative." "What is he trying to create?" "He wants to stimulate discussion." Step in his shoes and strive to discover his positive intent so that you can find your own as well! This is an essential piece of attitude and thought-mastery so that you

clear the slate for Real Conversations. The next step is to...

3. Take your notion of his positive intent and then reshape your judgment into what is called a "framing statement." "Help me connect the dots here." You can also formulate a question such as, "What was your thinking that leads you to come up with that solution?" Questions are powerful ways to build connection as you interact with others.

This practice works to transform how you approach difficult situations. It may seem awkward at first, and it may feel like not the right thing to do, but that resistance is a function of how your mind wants to be right about how wrong others are when you assume negative intentions. This is an effective way to put the pause button on your negative thinking so that you can create the possibility for a positive result to occur.

Assuming positive intent takes years of practice to master. In Jim Peal's book *Check Your Attitude at the Door*, you will find many tools that will help you get to Positive Intention. Assuming positive intent puts you in a positive frame of mind and gives whomever you are talking with the benefit of the doubt. Suspending your negative evaluation about that person helps you in many different ways. It opens up your mind so you can take a fresh look at the individual and the situation at hand. Positive intent neutralizes all of the non-productive, nonverbal signals you might be sending out in your communication. This prevents you from building a defensive or contentious environment. Assuming positive intent also creates a context for connection and partnership.

"Be kind whenever possible. It is always possible."
— Dalai Lama

GETTING TO POSITIVE INTENT:

1. Prior to a Real Conversation, notice what you are thinking and/or feeling. Are you in a negative mindset or do you have a positive attitude?

2. Stop for a moment and think about to whom you are going to talk. Ask yourself:

    • "In positive terms, what are/were they trying to accomplish? What am I trying to accomplish?"

    • "If they were able to achieve or behave in a way that would fulfill their positive intent, what would be different?"

    • "How would I respond differently if they were successfully achieving their positive intentions?"

3. Assuming their positive intent is authentic, create a scenario of how you would be thinking, feeling, and behaving. Step into that scenario in your mind's eye and reset your feeling state. (Taking a full breath often helps to release tension and reset negative feelings.)

4. If you find yourself already inside of a meeting and have not prepared with positive intent, you still can. Just run through steps 2 and 3 in your mind's eye, reset, and you will notice a shift. The more you practice, the better.

EXAMPLES OF SHIFTING NEGATIVE INTENT TO POSITIVE INTENT

Negative intent	Positive intent
1. "This person does not listen."	1. "This person is internally focused."
2. "This person is passive aggressive."	2. "This person needs a trusting environment to express."
3. "This person is dead wood."	3. "This person needs the right environment and motivation to improve."
4. "This person is stubborn."	4. "This person needs to commit."
5. "This person is defensive."	5. "This person needs a clear path and support to improve."
6. "This person is arrogant."	6. "This person needs to feel part of the team."

Bryan's boss interrupted him on a regular basis. "Yeah, I got it," he'd spout in the middle of Bryan's words. This was really irritating. "My boss doesn't like me." "My boss doesn't value what I have to say." "My boss is rude." "My boss is a bulldozer." These were thoughts that kept spinning through Bryan's mind. He realized he was in a negative loop. It felt like his boss was intentionally insulting his intelligence. Bryan stopped for a moment and thought, "I'm in a negative loop. If I shift a little into positive intent, I might understand what's going on. My boss has a lot on his mind, wants to get to the bottom line, and move on. He probably doesn't even realize he is cutting me off." This observation allowed Bryan to neutralize his negative feelings.

Bryan then imagined two scenarios:

1. He could calmly say, "I have two more points to cover" when his boss would inevitably interrupt.

2. He could initiate a discussion with his boss at a separate time about the interruptions from a place of neutrality.

Negative intent	Positive intent
1. "My boss doesn't like me."	1. "My boss and I have dramatically different styles."
2. "My boss doesn't value what I have to say."	2. "My boss has specific criteria that I need to discover."
3. "My boss is rude."	3. "My boss likes to openly brainstorm."
4. "My boss is a bulldozer."	4. "My boss has a high sense of urgency and drives to get to the bottom line quickly."

CONSIDER THIS:

1. List three negative reactions you have had to situations. What was the negative commentary inside of your head?

2. For each of the above situations, think about or create the positive intention for the other person or people.

3. Given that positive intention, craft a response based on positive intent.

Situation and negative self-commentary	What is their positive intent?	What is a way you can respond based on positive intent?
1.	1.	1.
2.	2.	2.
3.	3.	3.

"Expose yourself to your deepest fear;
after that, fear has no power, and the fear of freedom
shrinks and vanishes. You are free."
—Jim Morrison

GETTING THROUGH FEAR

Truth be told, Real Conversations almost always come wrapped in a veil of fear and doubt. All of your good intentions, skill sets, and practice will help you move forward, but they won't really take that fear away. Why? Fear is useful. It is actually your ally in this process. Fear speaks volumes by coursing through your body and making you stop and pay attention. It tells you that this Real Conversation is valuable, exciting, and important. Once you learn how to make fear your friend, you will listen to it and allow it to remind you that you need to take a breath, focus, and rise to the next level. Most of all, fear lets you know you are on the right track. Use this feeling as a catalyst to launch you into a new level of leadership and personal mastery.

Real Conversations require you to express and hear truths that you may feel are too risky to reveal or admit. Other common fears that spin through your mind include "I'll be embarrassed," "I'll look stupid," "I'll sound weak," "I'll be vulnerable," "I will get demoralized," and "Someone might get hurt and seek retribution." The list goes on and on. No matter who you are, no matter your position or authority, these kinds of seemingly irrational but real concerns will surface. In order to continually raise the bar and your leadership, you need to cut through your habitual fear mindsets to explore new ways of communicating. Having an open mind and an open heart is essential to being a good leader and will take you into a new level of leadership. Remember, showing your humanity to others and facing your own fears will not undermine your authority; it will actually strengthen your character and effectiveness.

Now that you know what Real Conversations are all about and how valuable they can be, you may wonder why the cat's got your tongue more often than not, and why you don't you feel comfortable telling it like it is or being open to hearing what someone has to say about you. This chapter poses one of the most important questions you will ever ask yourself: What stops me from having Real Conversations in at work? Discover the answers as you interact with a series of true-to-life stories that unreel typical situations you probably experience at your workplace.

We recently asked a large seminar audience this very question. We were amazed as we filled up over three huge flip charts with everyone's reasons or, as the group later admitted, excuses. It is amazing how many *seemingly* solid responses came up, internal comments and rationalizations that — once we looked at them rationally — were obvious attempts to avoid getting to the root of the matter.

We'll sometimes joke that the only valid reason for not having a Real Conversation is that your hands are tied and your mouth is taped shut! Of course, that is a tad cavalier. As we acknowledged in the Introduction, having Real Conversations does require strategic thinking, and there are times when the impulse to blurt something out is not actually in service of either person's best interests. This involves thoughtful discretion. But the bottom line is most of the "reasons" we run into over the years of working in organizations are, as they were with that audience, "excuses" in the end. Everyone is afraid to speak the truth and many are afraid to hear the truth. That's right. Regardless of how confident you are, you do have fears and doubts around Real Conversations, just like the rest of us.

Why? One reason that we have discovered is because most of us question whether telling the truth actually works. Usually, this fear of truth telling makes it pretty tough to engage in a casual conversation, let alone a Real Conversation. You might think you're not afraid. Or you might think you are being strategic. "Of course I'd never tell the whole truth," or "I'd get fired. I'm just being smart." You could go on and on. "What, am I crazy? They don't want to hear what I have to say." "In my office, everyone covers his or her tracks. I don't want to make waves." Underneath these responses there is fear. The fear may be valid, and it may not, but I need to tell you, the bottom line is that if you are like most of us, you frequently do not tell the truth because you really are afraid. And you are certainly not alone!

In a way, your mouth, or at least your heart and mind, is metaphorically taped shut. That is because you, and everyone else, are groomed to be wary of telling it like it is. You become paralyzed and can not seem to break through years of habitually shutting down and shutting up in front of what really needs to be expressed. And then what happens? Instead of going for it and having a Real Conversation, because you have no clue how, you find most of your energy is channeled into hiding your true thoughts and feelings.

Many are fearful that if you share your real self you will get into trouble—hell to pay later. Do you create a game face and masquerade around the office? Do you find some kind of cover-up behavior like being intimidating, distant, or curt to keep distance between you and the people with whom you work?

THE VEIL OF FEAR AND DOUBT

Granted, it can be scary to tell or hear the truth. The lump in your throat, knot in your stomach, or tension in your shoulders is a sign that you are experiencing what I call the "veil of fear and doubt." This is a poignant, visceral feeling that can catch you off guard. It wells up and surrounds you in its grip, but if you study it a little bit, you'll notice it is unpleasantly familiar. That's because it is a feeling based on one or more negative memories of what happened when you told the truth or someone said something to you.

Your veil of fear and doubt is actually a collection of sensations that jump out to warn you. "Don't say that! It might cause harm to you again. Bite your tongue. Something bad may happen!" This self-protecting mechanism literally comes to your so-called rescue and tries to keep you safe. This veil of fear and doubt is like the red flashing light at the entryway to most of the Real Conversations we want to have. Your challenge is to learn to expect the fear to show up, accept it, feel it, understand its message, and then move forward.

This is a bit of a steep learning curve because so many people have been deeply affected or worse, paralyzed by the fear that tells them to stop. While it is wise to identify "I am afraid," it is more important to understand what the positive intention of that fear really is. It does not mean do not tell the truth. It simply means look out, be careful. And very often you will instead interpret this as "Don't even think of going there. Don't say what you are really thinking or feeling because you'll get in trouble." Suddenly, you become ten years old and you are about to be sent to the principal's office or risk getting a spanking. Obviously, your responses are based on old stuff, stuff that no longer serves you.

While the majority of this book is about how to engage in Real Conversations, right now it is time to focus on the many debilitating costs inherent in beating around the so-called bush.

Beating Around The Bush?

Rate yourself on a scale from 1–10. Ask yourself:

- How often do I say what I am really thinking? (Vertical scale)

- How often do I ask the real questions that are on my mind? (Horizontal scale)

Before you get too attached to your score, you'll need to factor in another set of questions.

There are common communication behaviors that seem benign, but when studied a little more closely, are actually ways of manipulating a conversation. You might act like you are connecting with another person, but really you are controlling the conversation or keeping the other person at bay. There are endless ways to avoid having a two-way conversation, but without a two-way conversation, Real Conversations are just not possible. Which of the following three styles of communication ring true for you?

Are you a...

- Dominator

- Interviewer

- Disengager

Dominators: Say what they think without engaging others.

A dominating stance is often a defense for the fear of not having the right answer. This is a common tactic for those who do not want to be challenged. A leader will dominate with their opinion and take up all the space for other thoughts. This position extinguishes creativity and instills a culture of intimidation.

Ian, the leader of a research unit, gives his opinion to his team, tells them what he told them, and repeats himself. If someone dares to raise an eyebrow in question, Ian glares at them and talks louder. Ian is playing it safe. He never asks what anyone else thinks, and by dominating, he makes sure he never needs to explain himself or rise to a challenge. His team has learned to keep their ideas and suggestions to themselves.

Interviewers: Ask questions without voicing thoughts on the topic.

While asking good questions is a powerful practice, it can also be a defense for your fear of engaging in conflict, being wrong, or looking stupid. If you never state your opinion, no one can disagree with you.

Bill always asks a lot of questions. His interviewing technique provides him with an abundance of data and information. But in the debriefings after the weekly staff meeting, his senior staff executives fail to come up with a concrete understanding of Bill's position on any of the important issues. They are left in the dark while Bill beats around the bush and avoids taking a stand.

Disengagers: Often they look like they are preoccupied with something else. People may assume there is a hidden agenda or that the disengager is passive aggressive and withholding.

In staff meetings, William appears to be disengaged during the discussions and does not contribute to what is being said. Walt begins to wonder why William is not participating and questions whether he is truly a fit for his management team.

How often do you fall into the role of Dominator, Interviewer, or Disengager to avoid having to speak your truth and engage in a two-way conversation? Many organizations operate in a culture of fear and intimidation. Withholding information in any way can create a vicious cycle, which makes it more and more difficult to introduce any kind of freedom of expression. Secrets build on secrets and can become expensive, both financially and emotionally. These non-productive behaviors are a total waste of human resources and money.

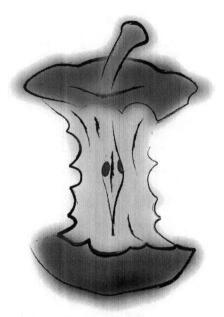

"I learned that courage was not the absence of fear, but the triumph over it. The brave man is not he who does not feel afraid, but he who conquers that fear."
— Nelson Mandela

THE THREE CORE FEARS

There are three fundamental fears. Which do you identify with most frequently? Or is it a combination of all three?

1. The fear of being rejected.

2. The fear of being alone.

3. The fear that something is wrong with you.

These core fears translate into a business context as:

- *I am afraid/concerned* I will look and/or sound stupid.

- *I am afraid* I will be ostracized.

- *I am afraid* I will look and/or sound weak.

- *I am afraid* I will be perceived as not being a team player.

- *I am afraid* of retribution.

No matter if you identify with one or all of these typical fears, you will soon be able to learn how to feel your fear(s), connect with them, and use them as your allies. This is not an impossible task, and the payoff is huge. Your fear will soon lose its power over you! So many people think that they need to annihilate their fears. Courage and confidence is the state in which you establish an honest relationship with your fear.

Fear is a natural part of being a human. Since you cannot eliminate it, why not use it as an accurate barometer that something challenging, risky, and new is happening or about to happen? It's time to have an honest Real Conversation with yourself about your personal fears. You can't have a Real Conversation with anyone else if you haven't had one with yourself. Once you open up the floodgates, you can move forward. Otherwise, your fears will continue to lurk in your body and mind and will keep you stuck and silent. Mastery of your fears will not make them disappear, but it will allow you to use the fear's energy to launch you into action instead of stopping you in your tracks.

The Positive Intention Fear

Years ago, Jim had some vivid encounters with his fear in an unforgettable recurring dream that came and went over a series of three or four months. Jim described the dream:

"In the dream, an ugly Cyclops chased me down a country road. I held a large sword, lashed out, and killed the Cyclops. But just as I was turning away, it came back to life and started chasing me again. I killed it over and over, but somehow it would always come back to life as soon as I turned away. The last time I dreamed about this Cyclops, I successfully hacked him into pieces and stuffed him into a huge metal trashcan. Like all of the other dreams, the moment I turned away he reassembled and started right after me.

"This time, though, instead of running, I stood my ground, looked him right in the eye, and asked, 'What do you want from me?' A giant tear dropped onto the ground and I heard him reply in the gentlest voice, 'I just want you to accept me.' In that moment, I felt a deep peace and knew that I had made a huge leap, one from resistance to acceptance. I learned by embracing what I was resisting that I could gain deeper confidence and more personal power. Now when fear comes up, and I assure you it does because it never really goes away, I directly ask it, 'What do you want from me?' Then I take a moment to really listen."

Fear is a part of life. You may be trying to destroy your fear in order to be fearless. This will never work. Confidence comes from confronting your fears and accepting them. Then fear will become your ally, not your enemy, and your life will change.

Making Fear Your Ally

How do you get started? How do you develop a relationship with a feeling? By having a Real Conversation with it, of course! With whom or what do you have a Real Conversation? With the voice of fear, that's who! How to begin? Before you start, please just be willing to give up a modicum of disbelief. Let your rational mind convince you the payoff is worth the process, and then put that reasoning mind aside. Most people that I have coached have one particular fear, or demon, if you will, that has become the basis of the beliefs they have spun around their sense of who they think they are. These beliefs then become the voice of negative intention or fear. As you speak to your fear, you will begin to identify the core story that lurks underneath your behaviors. Eventually the beliefs will begin to unravel and lose their hold over you.

The following story presents how a prominent leader faced, conversed with, and then embraced his fear so that he could finally express his truth.

Alex was anxious about talking to his team about an upcoming project that he saw as extremely challenging. In the preparation meeting, he paced and fidgeted.

His coach asked, "What are you so anxious about?"

He responded, "I am afraid my people will tune me out."

"May I coach you?"

"Yes."

The coach continued, "What is the positive intention of your fear?"

"What do you mean?"

"If you are concerned about your people tuning you out, the positive intention of your fear is to deliver a message that is clear and understood."

"That's right. I also want my team to engage in the direction I am setting."

"What do you need to do to be clear?"

"I think I just need to think this through."

"Great. Take a moment to integrate this insight."

As Alex thought about his insight, his expression softened and his shoulders actually dropped down. The coach suggested Alex have a conversation with his fear to see what it might teach him. After the coaching session, when the coach asked Alex if he wanted to rehearse what he was actually going to say to his team, Alex smiled and said, "No, I am ready." Once Alex was able to engage his fear and understand its positive intention, the fear became his ally and he regained his resolve.

In his opening comments, he spoke candidly, "It's been really uncomfortable for me over the past couple of months. I received some pretty serious feedback about my leadership and so I have been dreading this day.

"You see, originally I hired a group of consultants to evaluate the team, and I assumed they would help me understand why you all were having such trouble following my program. But instead, they came into my office and told me that I did not know how to lead! I was quite surprised and then rather depressed. It was not easy, but over time I realized I needed to change my focus. Usually I look at the facts. I had failed to focus on you, on my people! I was obsessing on bottom-line issues and did not recognize, nor could I acknowledge, the incredible value all of you bring to the company. I appreciate you, but I never had the courage to let you know that. I thought it would make me look sentimental or weak. And so to cover up that fear, I failed to sit down to get to know each one of you as individuals. I have seen my role as managing projects instead of working with and relating to people!

"Anyhow, when I was told my leadership was in question, I had to pause and re-prioritize. I know that within me it's not my nature to be a people person. This is an incredible stretch for me and I'm uncomfortable. But I'm working on it! I'm willing to do whatever it takes to make this team work."

As he spoke, he noticed people were relaxed, smiling, and responding in a positive manner. His vulnerability gave them permission to be open and vulnerable as well. His truth telling was transformational. It created more freedom for Alex the leader and for everyone in the organization. Alex learned how to walk through his veil of fear and doubt without being paralyzed. He took a risk, stepped out, and really made a breakthrough for himself and his company. This is what great leadership is all about.

Neutralizing Fears, Doubts, And Concerns

Sit quietly and close your eyes. Breathe three deep breaths. Think about how negativity shows up in your workplace. Think more specifically about how it shows up in your conversations with others. If it helps, focus on a particular incident and allow the feelings around it to come up and fill your body. You may feel your gut tightening, your shoulders tensing, your jaw clenching. Allow whatever is happening with no blame or judgment. Just notice.

Begin to have a conversation with your fear. Try not to edit your words. Go for it, even if it seems a little silly.

Here are some trigger questions to ask yourself to get you going:

Ask your fear, as if you are its coach, "What are you afraid of?"

Obviously, if this sounds too ridiculous, you might want to de-personify the emotion and just feel the fear and ask yourself, "What am I afraid of?"

The answer might come out in the form of "If ____ (event) were to happen, I am concerned that ____ (consequence) would happen." Fill in the blanks.

For example, you might say to yourself, "I am afraid that my boss will misunderstand me and that if she misunderstands, she will retaliate at the end of the year."

Track your physical and emotional sensations. You may want to write down some of your answers. Be honest with yourself. It may sound strange at first, but usually you are so busy listening to the voice of negative intention or fear that you assume that it is telling you the truth when it is actually putting up a wall and limiting your ability to grow as well as to connect to others.

With dedicated practice, you will begin to notice that when you have something important to do or say good old fear bubbles up, but now you will be able to identify it instead of doing its bidding. Over time, you might be able to interrupt the pattern for one second, then for two seconds, then for five minutes, and so on. In a short while, you will find you have a definite choice about how to use the fear as an ally instead of as a straitjacket.

As you begin to interrupt the negative intention cycle, you will initially feel uncomfortable, even defenseless in a way. That is because you are no longer defending yourself from feeling your feelings on a deep level. The goal here is not to panic and jump back to your old pattern of defending or moving into action. The goal is to STOP and BE with the fear. Take five again. Allow it to exist. Allow it to bubble up in your chest, make you short of breath, sweat, or panic a little. Give yourself some breathing room. Literally, breathe. This will feel odd, as if you shouldn't be doing it.

But this is the ticket, the breakthrough, the way out of fear and into enlivened expression and Real Conversations!

Breathing is a powerful tool needed to access and practice as you move through your fear. There is nothing more valuable than being able to tap into the natural processes we take for granted and use them to help slow down and transform our fear into a useful energy.

This may seem like unusual advice for a business-focused book, so bear with me for a few moments and try this out. Breathing gives your body and mind oxygen and releases carbon dioxide. It gives you a feeling of space, it centers you, and it allows you some room for hope and possibility. It opens you up. It melts the constriction fear creates, so instead of feeling "I'm afraid, I feel trapped, I don't know what to do," you can breathe and find yourself admitting, "I'm afraid, but I'm OK. I am all in one piece and I can choose. I have the space to be more powerful."

When you are in fear, you often hold your breath and escape into your spinning mind. One way to break this cycle is to locate the physical part of your body where fear lurks. "Where is it?" Typical locations are in the throat, chest, and stomach. Once located, close your eyes, inhale gently, and using your mind, move your breath into that area. Do this at least three times. Don't hyperventilate. Just gently inhale through your nose and gently exhale through your mouth. Sigh if you can, "Ahhhh." This is a process that is best done in a quiet place where you will not be interrupted.

By breathing into your fear and giving it room to be, you will begin to feel energized instead of depleted. Your body will also relax. Practice this type of breathing for a few minutes a day and you will notice a positive change. You'll soon be able to access this technique wherever you are, and move more and more easily from fear and negative intention to spaciousness and positive intention.

CONSIDER THIS:

1. To which of the following fears do you most relate?

    • *I am afraid/concerned* I will look and/or sound stupid.

    • *I am afraid/concerned* I will look and/or sound weak.

    • *I am afraid/concerned* I will be perceived as not being a team player.

    • *I am afraid of/concerned* about retribution.

2. What is the positive intention behind each fear? What needs to happen so that the fear has no basis?

3. What can you move toward or start doing to feel confident?

"Do exactly what you would do if you felt most secure."
— Meister Eckhart

"He that is good for making excuses
is seldom good for anything else."
—*Benjamin Franklin*

5 EXCUSES NOT TO HAVE REAL CONVERSATIONS

What stops you from having Real Conversations? The following five typical excuses are all born from fear and doubt, but have permutated into very specific, but predictable, responses. Notice how all of these excuses come from a place of negative intention.

1. **"There is not enough time."**
   This is the number one answer or rationalization that everyone offers.

2. **"Talking will not help. It will not make any difference."**
    This happens when we have given up and given in to our fears.

3. **"I do not have a concrete solution."**
    Leaders often feel that they can't enter into a conversation unless they know everything.

4. **"It will upset others."**
    Many people believe that it is fundamentally not okay to give somebody a message that might upset them. They assume the worst-case scenario: that what they say could be upsetting or worse.

5. **"It will open up a can of worms."**
    Nobody wants a mess, and people assume telling the truth is messy. This belief may come from memories of causing trouble when you opened your mouth or witnessed someone else opening theirs.

The following are more reasons (excuses) you may have for not speaking the truth.

- "No one is interested."

- "He or she will just get defensive."

- "This could negatively affect my performance review."

- "I'll become tongue-tied."

- "It's too emotional."

- "I don't trust anyone."

- "I don't feel there is enough rapport to be this vulnerable."

- "I have tried before and failed, so I don't want to go through that again."

- "This person is new; maybe I'll wait a while."

- "I've waited too long."

- "Well, if I wait just a little longer, I will have a new person to talk with, and I won't have to deal with this."

UNREAL AND REAL CONVERSATIONS AT WORK

The following stories are examples of how a variety of people in various business situations avoid Real Conversations, and then, after learning some practical skill sets, welcome and engage in them. Each illustrates the ubiquitous voice of negative intention. You will notice that when one person operates from this negative place, it is actually contagious. Since humans mirror one another, one voice of negativity creates another. In this way, a communication loop is created, one that needs to be undone before any Real Conversations can take place.

Listen for the stories and behaviors that resonate with your own patterns. Also notice how withholding the Real Conversation spins its own web of misunderstandings, innuendos, and inaccurate assumptions that accumulate and contribute to an entirely new set of problems and conflicts. Then review the UnReal and Real Conversation samples and notice how simple shifts in intention and language can make all the difference in the world.

Excuse 1: "There isn't enough time."

Tom has one-hour one-on-ones with his direct reports every other week. Although he physically shows up for the meetings, in his mind he is convinced he does not have enough time to have a Real Conversation with anyone. While the voice of positive intention is saying that there are some important performance issues that need to be honestly discussed, his voice of negative intention repeatedly insists loudly, "Tom, you cannot pull off anything in this limited amount of time. Who are you kidding?" Tom goes through the motions of talking with Fred about work objectives and milestones, but in the back of his head he is thinking about how Fred is not managing his time and failing to get the job done.

Fred, meanwhile, is chatting about his objectives, but in the back of his mind he is wondering why Tom is spending a whole hour going over objectives when Fred's real concern is about how to prioritize his projects so that he can get the most important ones done first. Fred's voice of negative intention is telling him that he should know which ones are the most important, and that he will look stupid if he asks questions. Fred senses that something is wrong; he feels that his boss is not telling him something, but he does not feel like he can ask about it. Instead, he imagines that his boss is going to lay him off in the near future. This worries Fred, and he frets about how he will have to tell his wife and the problems he will have trying to support his family without a job.

Here is part of the UnReal Conversation:

> Tom: "Fred, our time is a little bit short this week to go over your objectives. I thought it would be good if I just reviewed our objectives so you can be clear on what it is that you need to do."

> Fred: "OK, I guess that sounds fine. But..."

> Tom: "Why? Is there anything else that you wanted to discuss?"

> Fred: "No, I think we can just go over my objectives. We reviewed them at our last meeting and I think it would be useful again."

> Tom: "Well, is there anything that you are unclear about in your objectives?"

> Fred: "No, I think I'm pretty clear on what it is that I need to do."

> Tom: "OK. Well, let's just go ahead and review them then, and you can give me a progress update, and I think that will be that."

> Fred: "Fine, Tom."

Prior to the meeting, Tom had a private Real Conversation in his own head, but withheld it for fear of not having enough time to do it justice. What Tom does not realize is that Fred can sense that something is wrong. Fred, meanwhile, is spinning his own negative fantasy of what he thinks Tom is going to tell him. This negative fantasy is usually much worse than the real issue. It is an energy drain and performance inhibitor for Fred. If either party had ventured into the Real Conversation that was possible in the first place, they could have addressed real issues and come up with real solutions to both of their concerns.

Now, Tom and Fred open up a Real Conversation after learning some useful techniques. Tom takes a moment to focus.

> Tom: "You know, Fred, we have been having our bimonthly meetings and I've had this thought in the back of my head that I haven't really discussed with you. I think now would be a good time to see what we can come up with. Initially, I thought it would take too much time to get into it fully, but I figure we can at least begin, and if it takes more than an hour, we can schedule another meeting tomorrow or early next week."

> Fred: "OK. What is it?"

> Tom: "Well, it seems like I have spent a lot of time trying to clarify your objectives; however, I am really wondering if you feel you are getting your work done in the way you think you should. I want to hear your point of view. You see, it has

been a couple of months, and although I thought your priorities would be established and this confusion cleared up on its own, it appears that very little is changing. How can I help you figure this out?"

Fred: "Hmm. Well, one of the challenges that I have is getting a clear understanding of what is expected of me. What are my priorities? I know what the objectives are, and it seems as though I will start working on one and then I will get requests during the day to move things up or change the sequencing from my client base. And truthfully, I don't really have a sense of when to say no or when to say yes. And I guess in the back of my mind, I feel like I 'should' know what those priorities are, and in actuality I don't have a clue. I admit this is something I should have asked you a long time ago."

Tom: "Well, I'm actually glad to hear you say that because I didn't know if you were aware of what the difficulties actually were or if you thought that everything was fine."

Fred: "No, I actually knew that things weren't right, but I didn't know how to get it on the table in a way so that we could discuss it. Boy, am I glad that we are finally getting to the point here."

Debrief: By putting your real thoughts on the table, it actually takes less time to get through an issue, not more.

Excuse 2: "Talking won't help. It won't make any difference."

Sheila thinks that she had a Real Conversation with George, but all she did was beat around the bush. Her UnReal Conversation was vague and filled with innuendos and anecdotes about other people's problems. George, meanwhile, spent the entire meeting nodding his head. He did not want to interrupt her convoluted stories and, instead of being rude, kept quiet. Sheila, meanwhile, decided George is a passive aggressive personality because he never responds to what she thinks is communication.

Sheila failed to tell George that in her eyes he was being unresponsive. Each time she meets with him, she gets frustrated that he never seems to "get it." Meanwhile, George wonders why he has to meet with Sheila so often. In his mind, the meetings seem worthless.

George looks like he is a passive aggressive guy to Shelia but it is Sheila's reluctance to put the issue squarely on the table so that George can respond that sets him up to look that way. Shelia is not taking any responsibility for her inability to have a Real Conversation.

Here is part of the UnReal Conversation:

> Sheila: "You know, George, I was thinking about this conversation that I was having with a colleague of mine. And this colleague was really kind of stuck and didn't know quite how to make progress in this situation and so he actually hired

a coach. And this coach really helped this person get an understanding, and he really made some progress."

George: "Uh huh, OK."

Sheila: "So, it was one of those situations where this client of mine didn't quite understand how to engage fully in the work that was presented, and so the coach was actually quite instrumental in being able to provide some ideas and strategies."

George: "Oh. I see."

Now, here are Sheila and George after learning some useful techniques. Notice how they open up a Real Conversation.

Sheila: "You know, I was thinking about how we communicate together. I realized that at the end of our conversations, I'm usually left with a sense of frustration. I do a lot of talking and you nod your head, but I'm never sure what you're hearing or what kind of sense that it's making."

George: "Well actually, now that you mention it, you are right. I've been quite baffled because it seems like we don't focus on the business issues. I don't want to interrupt your stories, but I'm never really sure why you are telling me all of this stuff. To be honest...is it OK to be honest?" Sheila nods yes. "I do best when someone is direct with me. I need you to be direct with me, Sheila. The stories you tell are sometimes interesting, but usually I can't figure out why you tell them."

Sheila: "Thanks for that feedback. I thought my stories might be useful, but I can see how they have clouded the issue. It's true I have not been clear. From now on, I'll get right to the point."

Debrief: George and Shelia got to the point by putting what was in their left-hand columns, in their hearts and minds, out on the table.

Excuse 3: "I don't have a concrete solution."

Mary is excited and eager to attend a training to build her leadership skills. Tony knows she has been planning to begin her development courses for over two years, but sadly, there have been major cutbacks in funding. Tony is pretty sure that Mary may have to wait awhile to begin. His voice of negative intention tells him that if he raises the subject at all, he had better know all of the answers to her inevitable barrage of questions, and if he does not, he will not be doing his job adequately. He is worried about losing credibility, and also feels that he has to shield Mary from the training cutbacks. Tony's voice of negative intention tells him to avoid the topic at all costs because he is embarrassed that he does not have a specific way to move forward. He figures that if he cannot offer Mary the training program right now, then there is no use in having a conversation about her development.

Mary finds her conversation with Tony strangely uncomfortable. She assumes that since he has avoided talking about the training program, he does not care about her career. She figures that he is fast-tracking Brian, her peer, and that she will be left in the dust. She is beginning to wonder if she should return the call from the headhunter who called several weeks ago because she does not want to stagnate in her current position. Notice how many assumptions are made because of negative intention running the show.

Here is part of their UnReal Conversation:

> Mary: "I know it's only January, but I did want to get my plans in place. You know the leadership course is happening in October, and I want to make sure that everything is lined up."

> Tony: "Mary, although this hour has been set aside to discuss the development plan for this year, I think I'd rather go over some of our tactical plans and objectives. Since it is January, I want to get a jump-start on that, and then we can look at your development plan a little later on."

> Mary: "Well, OK. I just want to make sure that we talk about the training course and everything."

> Tony: "Well, I think it better that we focus on the work at hand."

> Mary: "I guess I will just put it on my calendar to talk with you later. When would be a good time?"

Tony: "Well, I think maybe the beginning of Q2 would be probably the best time to get around to talking about some development issues. Now let's talk about..."

Now, here are Mary and Tony after learning some useful techniques as they open up a Real Conversation.

Tony: "Hey, Mary, good to see you. Did you have a good Christmas holiday?"

Mary: "Yes, I did."

Tony: "Well, I'm really looking forward to working with you this year, and I've just been given some news that was disappointing. To be honest, I don't have a clear answer about how to address this, but I do want to have at least a preliminary discussion about it."

Mary: "OK. Well, what is it?"

Tony: "Well, I just got back from a meeting, and our numbers were way off Q4 last year. And so, what's happening is they are making cuts in all departments, and the number one area is around development training. Off-site training is not an option for this year. And I know that we had scheduled you to go to that leadership development course, and given the news I just got, that will not be happening. When I heard that, you were the first person who came to my mind because I knew how much you wanted to do that program. I wanted to let you know first-hand so that we can plan early for some alternative."

Mary: "Oh. Wow, that's really disappointing. OK. Well, I might need some time to think about what another alternative might be."

Tony: "OK. When do you think would be a good time to meet and actually discuss that? Let's brainstorm about it."

Mary: "How about in two weeks? That will give me some time to do a little research. It would be great to brainstorm with you."

Tony: "Yes, that's exactly what I wanted to do, just flag it up so that we could both kind of do some research and come back together. I will also do some research and find out what's available and within the budgetary realms of development because I definitely want to see you progress."

Debrief: When you have disappointing news to give, start your conversation by stating your positive intent and how the news impacts you as well. Telling the whole truth can be highly motivating. Tony learned that by including Mary in the process of finding solutions, he not only expresses his respect, but also promises to collaborate with her on bigger and better projects in the future.

Excuse 4: "It will upset others."

Fran has seen Susan leave Fran's meetings and instigate non-productive hallway conversations that undermine what was accomplished at the meetings. She wants to confront Susan about what Fran labels "disruptive" behavior. Fran is also disappointed that Susan is not much of a team player. Fran is hesitant to raise this issue because she fears that Susan will get angry, stew through another meeting, say nothing, and then go out and gossip again. Susan, however, believes Fran is giving double messages at meetings. This frustrates Susan, but her voice of negative intention tells her that it is not worth it to talk directly to Fran, who would label her as being difficult, and so gets it off her chest by complaining to her peers.

Here is part of the UnReal Conversation:

(Fran does not go to Susan but instead vents to her peer.)

> Fran: "I can't believe Susan. She is just upsetting the whole team but doesn't have the guts to talk to me directly."

> Peer: "Have you discussed this with her?"

> Fran: "No; she will just spread it around like she does with our meetings.

> Peer: "Now that you mention it, it does seem like she always has a sour face."

Now, here are Fran and Susan after learning some useful techniques, opening up a Real Conversation.

Fran: "Susan, I wanted to be able to take a few minutes to talk about some perceptions that I'm having and to find out what's happening on your side of things."

Susan: "OK...about what?"

Fran: "I'm not really sure what your experience is at our meetings. Usually you are very quiet and I have a hard time reading what is going on for you. Then I end up hearing what you chat about in the hallway after the meetings and discover how dissatisfied you are with what went on. I wanted to get an accurate perception from you rather than deal with hearsay. I hope we can discuss what is really going on."

Susan: "Wow, I didn't realize that I was creating that type of impression. It's true, I haven't been exactly happy here, and I know there have been times when I wanted to speak up and raise some objections, but I didn't. I felt like I'd upset everyone, and so I'd clam up and leave really frustrated. And maybe I did talk to people to just kind of vent a little bit, but I didn't mean any disrespect."

Fran: "Well, what have been some of your concerns? Let's take the meeting we had yesterday. Were there any objections there that you didn't have the opportunity to voice?"

Susan: "Well, actually yes, there were a couple..."

Debrief: Complaining and gossiping only create more negativity.

Excuse 5: "It will open up a can of worms."

Ed has observed Martha having emotional meltdowns during all kinds of meetings. She comes across as hyper-sensitive and takes everything personally. Ed has noticed Martha send clear nonverbal signals that let him and others feel like she just is not interested. It infuriates and frustrates him over and over again. Ed and others often respond by communicating with an edge in their tone of voice, and then Martha feels she is right about being persecuted.

Ed needs to confront Martha about a project that she is managing poorly. His voice of negative intention is telling him not to bring up her emotional shut-downs because he believes she will frame the whole conversation as Ed picking on her again. Martha notices Ed talking with and coaching her peers, but she feels singled out because he seems to avoid talking with her. She is angry that Ed seems to have his favorites, that she is being excluded from his inner circle, and that she is not benefiting from his advice.

Here is part of the UnReal Conversation:

> Martha: "I wanted to find out how the purchase orders are progressing for the supplies that I requested."
>
> Ed: "They are coming along and should be done next week. Is there anything else?"
>
> Martha: "No, I was just checking because one of my team members asked."

Now, here is how Ed and Martha, after learning some useful techniques, open up a Real Conversation.

> Ed: "I wanted to check out a few things with you about my leadership style."

> Martha: "OK."

> Ed: "I think that there are some ways that I can improve how we work together. If I could change one thing to be a better leader, what do you think I should change?"

> Martha: "Wow, Ed. Why are you asking me now?"

> Ed: "I sometimes get the impression that I could communicate better with you, but don't really know how that would be. I'd like some feedback."

> Martha: "Well, that's interesting. One thing that would make it better is if all the team members got the same opportunity to advance."

> Ed: "What do you mean? Can you be more specific?"

> Martha: "I certainly can..."

Debrief: In all of these stories, the people initially listened to their voice of negative intention. They do not consciously choose to, but years of habit simply kicked in. Negative intention can actually sound and feel like the truth, but it is not. Unfortunately, this pattern of going with what you know locks you into behaviors that are not coming from a place that can build clarity and connection. You need to realize that when you listen to your voice of negative intention and fail to identify and embrace the fear that lurks underneath, you end up undercutting your personal power in all situations.

"Fear is the cheapest room in the house.
I would like to see you living in better conditions."
—Hāfez

"You aren't learning anything when you're talking."
—Lyndon B. Johnson

TO "TELL" THE TRUTH?

One of the most interesting assumptions that guides, and limits, the effectiveness with which people carry out Real Conversations is the assumption that Real Conversations are about "telling" something. People often feel driven to have a conversation because there is something that they really "need to tell" the other person: feedback that "needs" to be given, or an opinion that "must" be expressed.

Paradoxically, it is often this very drive to "tell" the other person something that contributes to the conversation never happening, because equal to the internal drive to "tell," there is an internal concern that the other person won't take it well. "What if they get mad when I tell them?" Or "What if I hurt their feelings?"

Digging beneath these concerns, we can identify one of the most common barriers to having successful conversations: the mindset that "I am right, and I need to convince the other person that I am right." If you feel a strong need to "tell" the other person something, and you are very concerned about how they are going to take it, that is usually a sign that you may be putting more importance on your own view (and how "right" it is) than on what their view might be. You are concerned about their reaction because you are assuming that what you want to tell them is "right" and that it is important that they receive it.

Turning this assumption on its head opens up a new possibility for Real Conversations: what if I went in with the mindset that the other person doesn't need me to tell them anything? What if I assumed that their own intelligence and creativity will generate useful answers for themselves if I set up the conversation as a context for them to discover their own answers?

People are much more likely to remember and act on answers and insights that they generate for themselves than things they are told by someone else. If you can enter into a Real Conversation with this intention to serve the other person's learning process, rather than to "tell" them the answer you have learned for yourself, you have the possibility of creating a deep and sustainable discovery process — as opposed to an argument.

Here is a real life example of how one of these empowering, question-based Real Conversations happened. As you read it, notice how Gene refrains from "telling" Jason anything, but at each point asks questions to encourage Jason to apply his own intelligence and conclusions.

Jason, a corporate trainer, was co-leading a class with a colleague. While his colleague led a portion of the class, Jason went to the back of the room to listen and observe the participants. He pulled a spare chair from a table and perched up on the back of the chair, with his feet on the seat, in order to see his colleague at the front of the room over the heads of the participants.

Out of the corner of his eye he saw Gene, one of the Health and Safety team members, rise from his seat and approach him from the side. Gene quietly said, "Jason, I'm gonna have to ask you to come down off the back of that chair, please."

Jason got down immediately, feeling embarrassed that he'd called attention to himself in this way, and very aware that he was sitting on the chair in an unsafe way.

Gene continued: "Do you have a sense of why I asked you to come down?"

"Yeah," said Jason. "As soon as you mentioned it, I realized it was unsafe."

Gene nodded in agreement. Then he continued to explore the scenario: "What's the worst thing that could have happened?"

Jason looked down at the smooth, hard floor, and looked back at Gene: "Well, worst case I could have fallen backwards and really cracked my head there."

Smiling all the while, and staying very nonjudgmental, Gene continued, "And what impact would that have had on others?"

"Wow," Jason said, actually feeling the potential impact as he began to answer. "I would have caused quite a disruption to the course, which would affect everybody. And I'd be really letting my colleague down if I was unable to continue." He thought he was feeling embarrassed at first, but now he was blushing.

"And your family?" added Gene, still smiling supportively.

"Yes, if I seriously hurt myself here that would be a huge letdown for my family right now. They need me healthy."

"All right, good," said Gene. "I hear that you are really thinking through the potential implications of your action, and I appreciate that. I also know you well enough to know that you had some good reason for sitting up on the back of that chair. What was your positive intent?"

Now Jason felt a surprising lift inside. Instead of feeling embarrassed, he began to appreciate how supportive Gene was being. He wasn't being reprimanded or scolded; he was being trusted and encouraged, and it felt good. He smiled now, as well. "Well, I wanted to see over the heads of the participants and make sure that Brian, in the front of the room, could see that he had my full attention and support."

Gene: "That's great. So you wanted to support your teammate and have a good view from the back of the room. Can you think of any other alternatives for meeting those objectives that would be safer?"

Jason: "Sure. I'll bet they have high stools in this place; I could ask for a stool to sit on. That would actually be much more comfortable, anyway."

Gene: "Great, sounds like you have a new plan. One last thing: what can I count on from you in the future?"

Jason smiled sheepishly again: "Well, for one thing you can be sure that I won't sit up on the back of an unstable chair like that again. But more than that, the way you handled this with me has really allowed me to see that I just don't think proactively about safety. So you can count on me to think much more proactively and carefully about safety conditions from now on. Thanks, really. The way you trusted me to come up with my

own answers has really made this whole conversation sink in deeper for me."

Gene could have simply TOLD Jason to get off the chair and
to try something else. He could have TOLD him what the
worst-case implications were and that Jason wasn't taking
safety seriously enough. That's what we usually do. And if
he had done so, Jason probably would have listened, and
would probably have agreed with some of it, and would
probably have discounted or disagreed with other parts
of it...like most feedback conversations we enter into. And
what we can guess is that the impact of that conversation
would have been minuscule. Jason would have avoided sitting up on the back of the chair for the rest of that training,
but it is doubtful that he would have taken Gene's words
and applied them further than that. A normal human response would be that in the very next training, he'd look
around, make sure Gene wasn't there, and sit up on the
back of another chair!

But the impact of this Real Conversation was much greater than that. Because Gene utilized an approach of asking Jason to do his own thinking, and gently affirmed and
supported Jason's answers, he created the possibility for a
much deeper learning. Jason went forward with a deeper
awareness of safety and the potential implications of his
own choices. He noticed many other situations, similar to
sitting up on the back of a chair, in which he took safety
risks that he had never noticed before. He learned more
from Gene's "asking" than he ever would have from being
"told."

Now, what Gene did successfully was not simply a matter of "asking" as opposed to "telling." We all have had questions asked of us that did not feel particularly supportive or encouraging. The key to what made this Real Conversation so masterful was not merely the behavior of "asking," but that it started with the assumptions Gene was making before he even opened his mouth. As opposed to the more limiting assumption we mentioned at the beginning of this chapter ("I am right and I need to tell this other person so they'll understand..."), Gene was operating with a positive belief that Jason would be able to apply his own intelligence and positive intentions. This empowering assumption, and the encouraging behaviors that flowed from it, made the Real Conversation easy for Jason to fully take part in. There was nothing to resist or defend, only a supportive invitation to do his own thinking and discovery on the issue.

"Conflict is the beginning of consciousness."
—M. Esther Harding

SHRINKING YOUR BLIND SPOT—REQUEST FEEDBACK

You have blind spots. Everyone does. Blind spots exist in all areas of your life. It is obviously a challenge to identify them, but it is important to build an awareness of what you typically do not see or know when you are engaged in having a Real Conversation. Communication is the way you share information, insights, and ideas that help you achieve business goals and make a positive difference. A Real Conversation is one in which you get to the point and create the intended impact.

As you learn more about having Real Conversations, you will discover that there is often a huge discrepancy between what you intend your message to be and the message received. Although you may be clear about the intent and substance of your communication, you might be surprised at what others hear or interpret once you open your mouth!

Stan, the new IT vice president of a fast-growing company, called a meeting of his executives to help him get up to speed on their current projects. Stan eagerly anticipated the visual presentation, but the PowerPoint support materials were filled with glaring spelling errors. Obviously disappointed, Stan looked directly at the presenter and said, "This presentation is not at the level necessary for these meetings or for any presentation in our department. I expect all of our presentations to be free of spelling errors."

Stan felt his communication was clear and effective, but this particular organization did not practice communication that was so obviously direct and open. Everyone was used to operating in private; being critical in front of others was considered a serious confrontation. The hallway rumor mill spoke of Stan as "being on the attack," and "tearing the presenter apart and ruining his career." To complicate matters, since the business culture was nonconfrontational, no one told Stan about the negative force of his words. Stan could have defended his comments by simply stating that he expressed a straightforward, unemotional, realistic expectation, but that is not how he was heard. What Stan intended is not what was received.

It is important to ask yourself if the way that you think you are communicating is the way you are actually being heard. Do you know for sure? Are you making the kind of impact you want to make? Where are your blind spots?

Blind spots are a function of your nervous system. Seven to ten billion bits of information stream into your nervous system each and every moment. Can you imagine what it would be like if you were actually consciously aware of all of that? That is a lot of information! Think about the wide-open look on the face of an infant whose nervous system is totally open to all the millions of bits. "Seven to ten million bits...I've got to sleep...I'm tired...I'm hungry... Someone change my diaper...I need a break." No wonder they sleep so much.

As your nervous system developed, it formed two aspects of awareness. The conscious mind is very much like the tip of an iceberg, floating above the vast, usually shadowed unconscious mind. The conscious part is like a spotlight. It allows you to pay attention to something specific, something particular, happening in this very moment. Right now, for instance, you are aware of the words on the page, perhaps you hear the sounds in the room, but you are probably not aware of what your tongue is doing. Ah, now you are. That is because the word triggered a specific part of your conscious mind to focus on the content "tongue."

You can choose to direct your spotlight of conscious awareness to different parts of your experience. You can choose to identify and ultimately shrink your blind spots. Sound like a paradox? Well, once you are aware you have a particular blind spot, you will begin to develop a way to actually identify, locate, and diminish it. To shrink your blind spot you need to be receptive to what is going on in the moment. There are verbal and nonverbal clues about what is really happening, and they need to be seen before you can shrink your blind spot, and then re-educate your awareness to be open and alert to seeing and using all of the feedback available.

Cheryl was passionate about her work. As the manager of store operations, she had a great sense of urgency and wanted to tackle problems head on. What Cheryl did not realize is that her intensity would often shut down the people who worked for her. "You have got to jump on that right now." "I need that done yesterday." "Are you racing the glacier today?" These comments usually fell on deaf ears. Her staff experienced her comments as urgent pressure instead of a playful incentive to encourage their best efforts.

Cheryl's tremendous focus on her goals tended to overshadow the impact of her style and created a blind spot that got in the way of her being heard and understood. She failed to notice people's nonverbal, but obviously negative, reactions to her communication. She needed to learn how to shrink her blind spot so that she could pay attention to cues people were giving her and incorporate those into her awareness while communicating with them.

Generous listening means that you listen not only with your head, but also with your heart and gut. So often when you listen, you are stuck inside your head rehearsing what your next line is going to be. Preparing allows you to put your full attention on the other person. Then you can listen in between the lines as well and hear the subtext that is carried in the tone and emotion of the other person's words. Keep in mind about 90 percent of the meaning of a person's communication is expressed in how he says his words and what he does with his body.

Mary is adept at really listening at all levels. "I am hearing something that sounds like a deeper concern you might be having, but I am not sure what it is. Do you have another issue that you haven't addressed? Is there something else on your mind?"

When you pay attention with all your senses, you can glean a lot of information. It requires that you put aside your agenda and "be present." Generous listening does not mean that you will not get to your points, but rather it means that you fully listen first. This also sets the model for others to listen to you.

There are many practices that can help you listen generously. Periodically stop the person and say, "I want to make sure that I understand what it is that you are saying." Then feed it back and watch for the nonverbal yes or no that she gives you. Ask, "Is there anything that I'm missing? Is there anything that you want to add to that?" Make sure you have really mined what it is that she wanted to communicate. Also, make sure that you are understood. Here are the key questions:

- What is your understanding of what I have covered so far?

- What is the impact on you?

- What further questions or concerns do you have?

"Always take hold of things by the smooth handle."
— Thomas Jefferson

WELCOME FEEDBACK

You are always getting feedback from whoever it is with whom you are communicating. The question is, are you noticing, taking in, and responding to their many responses, both verbal and nonverbal? You may hear the words that are spoken, but nonverbal messages are often missed. For example, how focused are you on the way someone wrinkles her brow, frowns, crosses her arms in front of her chest, or tilts her head? These gestures reveal how you are impacting her. Notice and pay attention. If you are so focused on yourself, you will miss these revealing signals.

It was not easy for a fast-moving person like Cheryl to learn how to open her awareness and look at her blind spots. She began by first developing the ability to observe and then articulate what she was seeing in her associates' behavior. Cheryl began to pay attention to people's eyes. Were they alert or were they glazed over? She learned how to listen to their words as well as the gaps between the words. Did they chuckle nervously? Were they sounding resigned or enthusiastic?

Then Cheryl cultivated the ability to check in with her people to find out what they were thinking in that very moment. For example, Cheryl began to notice reactions to what she said and would respond with, "You seem preoccupied..." Or "It seems like you have a question about what I just said. What can I clarify?" Or "It seems like I am not making my communication clear. What did you just hear me say?" Cheryl was actively opening her eyes to her own blind spot. This intention helped her enter, or re-engage, in what was about to become a Real Conversation. Notice that in the examples above Cheryl first articulated what she was seeing in a non-defensive way ("It seems like you have a question about what I just said") and second, added a question at the end as an invitation for a response ("What can I clarify?").

The people who worked with her noticed that she was paying attention to them and they felt seen, heard, and respected. In turn, they were able to communicate what they needed in that moment. Cheryl's new behaviors enhanced her leadership impact. The more she was willing to be open and create these productive communication exchanges, the easier it was for her to shrink her blind spots to make room for more Real Conversations.

WILLING TO BE COACHED?

Shrinking your blind spot is also a function of your commitment to receiving feedback. The key here is being willing to be coached. By assuming positive intentions in others you can relax your mind and hear, in an open and receptive way, what somebody has to say to you. If you want to be effective at giving feedback to others, then you need to be excellent at receiving feedback. It isn't always easy, but it is worth learning. As you learn how to request feedback and actively engage in shrinking your blind spots, you will develop the courage to cut through the veils of fear and doubt as they come up.

Stephen learned how to request feedback from his direct peers in a friendly manner. Walking down the hallway or at lunch, he'd casually make a request: "Hey, Gloria, let's go for a five-minute walk. I'd like to get some input about how I've been working with you lately." During the walk, he'd ask, "How am I doing? If I could change one thing to be more effective in the way I communicate and interact with you, what would that be?"

Asking for one thing that you could do to improve your leadership puts feedback in a positive context. That's much different than asking, "Tell me what my strengths are," or "Tell me what my weaknesses are." Why? Because listing strengths and weaknesses sets up polarities that inevitably put focus on the negatives. That is just how it works. Again, when you ask, "What's the one concrete thing that I can do or change to be better?" everything is put into a positive context. This is the type of environment that you want to create around feedback.

Feedback is given to support people to achieve excellence. The more that you can model Stephen's style of asking for input, the more you will receive constructive feedback that will certainly upgrade and impact your work. A simple request for feedback on a regular basis can be profound. Make sure you follow comments with a validation of what you heard. Always respond with something like, "OK, let me clarify. What I heard you say is..." Remember that since you are requesting the feedback, there is nothing to defend.

You do not have to wait until something is wrong in order to get feedback. In fact, as you begin to proactively seek feedback on a regular basis, you will see that your own performance improves a whole lot more than if you waited until your annual performance review. Ask for feedback from everyone with whom you work. It can be a quickie five-minute exchange. Once you get used to it, it becomes easy. "Hey, I just want to check in with you again. You know, a couple of months ago I asked you how I was doing and you gave me that one great tip about listening without interrupting. How have I been doing with that? Is there anything else I could do to be more effective in working with you?"

One of the keys to requesting feedback is keeping the list focused. You do not need to get a whole laundry list of issues and problems. Take one thing you want to work on and ask each person on your team what he or she thinks. You may see that there is a trend, and out of all of the people that you ask, you might find that there are three things you could do to be more effective. Then, simply focus on accomplishing those three. Now you are really taking charge of your growth and development!

"Intense feeling too often obscures the truth."
— Harry S. Truman

HOW TO RECEIVE FEEDBACK

I f you find yourself feeling defensive when you listen to feedback, a few simple sentences that you can memorize and use will make all the difference. Take a time out. You can say, "Hold on a minute. I just need a moment to put my ears back on so I can hear this," or "Hang on just a second. I wasn't expecting this and need a moment to shift gears to really hear you," or "Could you repeat that again? I notice that I just checked out there for a moment and I really want to be able to hear what it is that you have to say."

Robert, a highly respected district sales manager, asked me, "What should I do if I think the person who is giving me feedback is a complete idiot?" My response was simple: "Remember that they have a positive intention for you. This will help neutralize your negative attitude and negative nonverbal cues you might be sending to that person."

When someone gives you feedback, here is a list of questions you can use to clarify their input:

- What specifically happened?

- What was the sequence of events?

- How did that impact you?

Ask these questions with the intention of understanding the person's experience rather than making her wrong. After you have heard her message, all you basically need to say is, "Thank you. This is what I heard you say..." You do not have to respond to it. You do not have to tell her what you are going to do with the feedback. Simply receive the message and tell her, "I'm going to think about what you have said." This is the artful and graceful way to receive feedback. When Robert adopted this type of response, the two "idiots,",in his eyes, he did not want to hear from, as if by magic, stopped being so ignorant and actually became valuable sources of input and information.

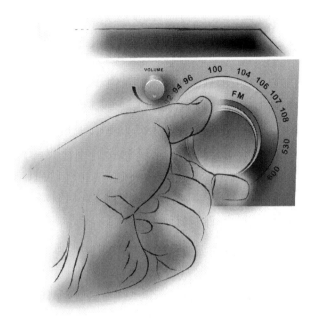

"The best way to find out if you can trust somebody is to trust them."
—Ernest Hemingway

GROWING RAPPORT AND TRUST

Rapport operates from the principle of "like likes like." For some, rapport is a natural process for others, rapport takes conscious effort. Creating rapport is different from mechanically mimicking somebody. Mimicking creates discomfort and ridicule. Rapport brings you into a shared experience so that both of you are comfortable. How do you create rapport? Express a similarity between yourself and whoever you are with using the following three elements of communication:

1. Body postures and gestures

2. Voice, tone, and tempo

3. Key words and phrases

When you have rapport, there is a very natural flow; there is a mirroring of each other's bodies and a matching of voice tones, quality, tempo, and emotion. As you create rapport, notice what the other person is doing and begin to bring some of his behavioral characteristics into your behaviors. If he speaks with a quiet voice and you normally speak with a loud voice, bring your voice volume down a little bit to match his. If he uses big gestures, take on using some larger gestures. Do all of this in a way that feels natural for you. Always keep your eye on doing something that is similar to what he is doing with his body, gestures, and with the tone and tempo of his voice. This will keep the pipeline of rapport open and create a much greater bandwidth for your communication to take place.

YOU ARE NEVER TOO POOR
TO PAY ATTENTION

Many attempted communications go sideways because you are not paying attention to the signals the other person sends your way. Steve, a sales representative, managed to get a short meeting with one of the Key Opinion Leaders (KOL) in his district. Within seconds, Steve was dumping information on him in a rapid-fire style. Steve was so busy trying to get all the information out that he did not realize the KOL was looking at his watch every few seconds. After three minutes, the KOL said, "I'm sorry, I have to go. I have patients waiting," and he stood up and walked out of the office.

Steve did not understand why the KOL left so abruptly. Simply put, Steve missed his opportunity to engage him. He failed to pay attention to the signals he was sending. Why? Steve was so excited about dishing out his data that he was not fully present. If he were, he would have recognized his time was limited and it was necessary to be sensitive to the other person's needs.

In order to be fully present, you need to quiet the internal distractions that pull you away from the business at hand. There are three things you can do become fully present:

1. **Listen Generously:** Drive the other person's agenda. Find out what is important to the other person and use that as an entry point. Had Steve started his meeting with "Since we have just a few minutes, what would make this meeting valuable for you?" he would have engaged the KOL right off the bat. You gain much more leverage and influence by starting where the other person is rather than forcing your ideas upon them.

Listening generously requires that you suspend the type of thinking that creates pressure. Limited time is the usual thought that will stop you from listening well. When you are thinking about what to say next, you are not paying attention and others will feel like you are forcing something on them. They will often deflect your efforts to convince them, and then you fail to build a relationship. When you stop and truly listen, you create a different dynamic. Instead of one person making their point and the other countering, you enter into more of a collaboration of ideas. Listening generously allows you to model the behavior you want to employ in the relationship.

2. **Prepare well:** In order to have a successful interchange, it is important that you prepare so that you can be present; otherwise, the anxiety of what you might forget will consume your mind and your meeting.

Martha was anxious about a presentation that she was going to make to a group of senior executives. Her internal voice kept telling her that she didn't know the details well enough to field questions. Rather than continue feeling anxious, she asked herself, "Which details do I not know well enough?" She quickly came up with three areas that she did not feel adequately prepared for, did her homework, and that nagging voice transformed into a voice of confidence.

3. **Notice, name, and ask about nonverbals:** Lu paid a lot of attention to other people's nonverbals but realized she was more absorbed in observing than in being present. She eventually learned how to articulate what she was seeing and then asked her team for confirmation. When Lu saw someone flinch, furrow their brow, gulp, or roll their eyes, she'd gently say, "I just noticed you furrowed your brow. I am wondering, what are you thinking?" "I noticed a different tone in your voice, and I am wondering what that means." This practice not only allowed Lu to be fully present, but her prompts initiated more personal conversations and opened up the discussion to the real issues at hand.

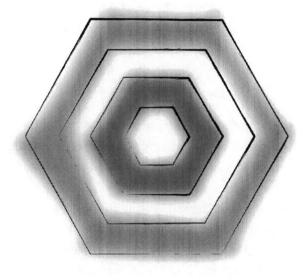

REAL CONVERSATIONS WITHIN
REAL CONVERSATIONS

Being present is one of the fundamentals of Real Conversations. Being present is a combination of noticing what is going on and being able to articulate and integrate into the conversation what you perceive while it's happening. Once you launch into a Real Conversation, other issues may arise. These are what I call Nested Real Conversations. By being present, you can read the nonverbal cues that the other person is sending and you will know that there is another hidden topic to discuss.

Juan learned to pay close attention to nonverbal behaviors. When he noticed a brow furrow or tension in the other person's jaw, he would stop and say, "I just want to hear what you are thinking right now," or "How is what I am saying impacting you?" By injecting these inquiries, he could engage in the Real Conversations that were just below the surface. By immediately engaging a person when you notice a visible nonverbal response, you keep the conversation real and in the present.

Adapted from the Johari Window

GROWING YOUR PUBLIC OPERATING SPACE

There are three primary ways to enhance or grow your Public Operating Space. The first is to learn how to put the ideas from your "Business Personal Zone" on the table. The second is to build trust, and the third is to cultivate an open mind.

The Business Personal Zone is what you are thinking or feeling about a particular business issue, but haven't made public yet. It is your job to get the Business Personal things out on the table.

"Private" refers to the things about you that you may communicate to your friends or someone you are in a relationship with or maybe just keep to yourself. Some people have a very distinct boundary line between what is Business Personal and what is Private. People you work with for years may have disclosed very little about what is Private for them. Some people are the open-book type and will tell you everything: their bank balance, their relationship status, or their health problems. It is important to respect where each individual draws his or her line. Regardless of where you draw that line for yourself, it is your job to identify and make sure you get your own Business Personal Zone ideas out on the table in a way that moves things forward.

Most of the time there is a running commentary in your inner thought bubble (Business Personal and Private) that you are constantly editing when you want to communicate (Public Operating Space). Is this a blessing or detriment?

Tony, a director, was at ease saying whatever was on his mind with spontaneity and vigor. Sometimes people were shocked by his blatant openness, and consequently, people either loved him or hated him. From Tony's point of view, he was just being himself.

Sandy had major objections to her boss Jerry's execution plan, unreeled at a recent meeting. She thought of at least three factors that could be major obstacles to the success of the project. Sandy did not want to disrupt Jerry's presentation but was eager to share her concerns. She was at a choice point; she could hold the ideas in her Business

Personal Zone to herself or put them on the table. Sandy decided to wait until she could talk privately with her boss rather than share her objections in public. She balked and gave into her fear of not knowing how her boss might respond to a public objection. Her choice meant not sharing her expertise and valuable point of view in the moment. This may have cost the organization time because the others in the meeting may have walked away and taken action based on what was said.

Building Trust — Share Something Personal That People May Not Know About You (Open The Kimono)

Stan opened his team retreat meeting with a slideshow illustrating the highs and lows of his personal and professional life. Everyone enjoyed gleaning insights into the events that shaped his character. The more that someone knows about you, including your passions, hopes, and fears, the easier it is for them to trust you.

Business is not an exclusive arena; it is a human forum. Sharing what makes you tick, getting up close and personal to your team, builds a bond that allows enhanced relationships and more successful business endeavors.

Corey, an executive leader in manufacturing, told his team, "One of the areas that I'm working on is fully listening to what people have to say instead of cutting them off in mid-sentence. I admit that I do that a lot. So if I interrupt and I don't catch it, please let me know so I can hear your whole thought."

When you engage others in helping you out, you give them the chance to come through, and the dynamic of the exchange will benefit everyone.

Selected stories from when you were growing up are very powerful when you talk about yourself in a team context. What did you learn from your parents? Revealing what formed your core values and home life lessons lets people know more about your character.

- What values did your mother/father/grandparents instill in you, and how have you applied them?

- Who was a hero in your life, and why?

- What was a major disappointment that you had in your life?

- What was something that really hurt you in a business context? What did you learn?

It can also be something personal. When my daughter was a little infant she had asthma and I literally was up all night, holding her so she could breathe. Funny how it works. You stay up all night and then in the morning the kid is better. It's like, "Hi, Daddy," while I am fast asleep and snoring. That could be just letting the person know why you are so grumpy or edgy. It is because you have been up all night.

These kinds of stories provide a powerful backdrop to your current concerns as a communicator and leader. The more you tell your story in an open and authentic way, the more comfort people around you will have with you, and the more they will grow to trust you. Most leaders who share these types of stories often doubt the value of telling them before the fact and then are convinced of their value after they see the amazing response.

The above diagram illustrates two people attempting to have a Real Conversation. Notice how the independent circles that represent "You" and the "Other Person" gradually move toward each other and overlap.

The end result represents a situation in which what you know and what I know is basically equal. The intended impact of this very Real Conversation is the actual result!

It is possible to create this kind of solution by growing the size of this overlap, the area that I call the "Public Operating Space." In each of your relationships, you have a certain degree of Public Operating Space; in some it's far greater than in others.

Tom and Susan have been working together for five years. If you were to overhear their conversation, it might sound like they were being rude.

> Susan: "That was a pretty dumb idea. Can't you get both brain cells to fire?"
>
> Tom: "Stupid is in the eye of the beholder. I rest my case."
>
> In fact, these two have a deep level of rapport and trust between them.
>
> Tom and Fred sometimes yell at one another as they are discussing an idea, but this is normal for them. (They have learned to close their doors so others aren't upset!)
>
> Tom: "You have got to be kidding if you think we can meet that timeline."
>
> Fred: "I don't know what your problem is. This IS what we HAVE to do. It's not an option so get over it."

Again, it sounds like these associates are having a fight, but they have created an energetic style of communication as comrades who really know one another. These two examples illustrate people who trust one another and have found a communication style that works for them both. Trust is the key principle necessary to build and expand the Public Operating Space. It supports a place where you can say what you are thinking. If there are any misunderstandings, you can clear them up quickly and move on. Real Conversations increase the Public Operating Space. When this space is as large as possible, it gives you the greatest amount of freedom to communicate, be productive, and have more Real Conversations!

> *"I expect to follow my instincts of openness
> and candor with full confidence that honesty
> is always the best policy in the end."*
> **—Gerald R. Ford**

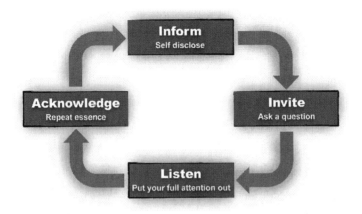

"There is no such thing as a worthless conversation, provided you know what to listen for. And questions are the breath of life for a conversation."
—**James Nathan Miller**

THE CONVERSATION CYCLE

Certainly you have been in that situation where the other person just wouldn't shut up, it was all about them, they just kept on talking about themselves and never created the space for you to contribute to the conversation. Remember the time when it seemed like the other person was just interrogating you with a barrage of questions? Or talking with someone who it multitasking? How about the person who was trying to understand but never quite made it?

The above are examples of situations where people were not having a balanced conversation. Real Conversations have a natural flow through various modes and exchanges.

In particular, when conversations are going well there is a balance of these four modes:

- Informing—sharing about your point of view

- Inviting—asking the other(s) to share

- Listening—eyes, ears, and mind attentive to who you are talking to and what they are saying

- Acknowledging—feeding back the essence of what you have heard so others know they have been heard.

So often we're in a situation where the other person over informs. In other words, they get stuck on telling their story. It's really not a conversation in that case; it's more of just you sitting there listening, waiting for your turn to talk and never getting it. Keep that in mind when you have a lot to say or you think you have the immediate answer to somebody's problem; you want to engage them in a conversation. Make sure that after you inform that you create the space for them to talk by asking a question—inviting.

Likewise, you've been in a situation where somebody's just firing questions at you. Each response you give is followed by an immediate new question. How annoying, or even unsettling, can that be? It comes across more of an interrogation than a conversation. Remember that after you ask your question you want to follow through the rest of the conversation cycle to create a balanced flow—really listen to the answer provided, and let the other know that you've been listening by acknowledging what you heard. Then, if you still have another question or two, your conversation partner at least knows that you have heard what they have said so far.

Listening means putting your full attention on the person. We've all been in the situations where we were listening to the person but doing something else — multitasking. The problem with multitasking is that it's really a very inefficient way to have a Real Conversation. In fact, it makes having a Real Conversation impossible. You'll find that you'll get a lot further in conversation by really giving somebody your complete attention.

The fourth stage, acknowledgment, means simply to let the other know that you have heard them. Jumping immediately into your own story or thought as soon as they are finished is often a sign that you were NOT actually listening, but already rehearsing what you wanted to say next. When you take the time to reflect back what you have heard, you not only honor the person who has been speaking with your attention, but you also create a chance to check out whether how you understood them actually matches what they intended to say.

There are many, many different ways to acknowledge what you have heard, from the simple head nod or single-word assurance ("Sure") to repeating back the exact words you have heard the other say. Many of us have been taught to acknowledge by translating what we have heard into our own words. There are times and places where this works best — especially when we want to test whether or not we have understood. But when you are using the acknowledgment mode to really let the other person know that you are listening and that they have been heard, then the most direct route is to simply use their words.

One very elegant way to acknowledge what you are hearing from another person is to listen carefully for their "key words." Each of us have words that have particular meaning or valence to us, and we tend to use these words frequently, or to set them apart with extra emphasis in our tone. By noticing and reflecting back another person's keywords, you join with their patterns of speech and thought and feeling more fully.

You can experiment with different ways to use the acknowledgment stage of the conversation cycle, and see what works best for you. We have found over the years that different people like to give and receive acknowledgment in different ways, and it is helpful to learn which ways work best with your own colleagues. The same goes for the other modes of the conversation cycle. When conversation is easy and the relationship is strong, we tend to cycle through the different modes naturally, without effort. But when we are intending to create a Real Conversation where there has not been that kind of ease, consciously attending to the balance of informing, inquiring, listening, and acknowledging can be a great foundation of support.

"Everything in life is speaking in spite of its apparent silence."
—Hazrat Inayat Khan

THE POWER OF SILENCE

You are probably all too familiar with the sayings "Silence is golden," and "It is better to be seen and not heard." More than likely, frustrated parents created these clichés to keep their children quiet and controlled. Although drummed into your head decades ago, these words may still reverberate and affect why you choose to keep quiet rather than speak out. It is difficult to imagine an employee and/or leader making a significant contribution by "being seen and not heard." Just as words can be constructive or destructive, the same theory applies to silence.

There are so many different kinds of silence. Consider the pregnant pause, getting the silent treatment, or being choked up and unable to speak, to name a few. Shutting down and being silent is often a knee-jerk response. Consciously choosing when to speak and when not to speak is a skill you want to cultivate. Silence is a seasoning that can enrich your communication, but is not meant to be the main course, especially if you want to have Real Conversations. There are many kinds of silence, but when it comes to having a Real Conversation, three are pivotal to understand:

- Withholding Silence: when you are holding back your important messages

- Silence of Compliance: when you are not speaking up to be politically correct

- Intentional Silence: when you use silence on purpose to empower a situation

Withholding Silence — Silence Is Not Passive

Bob, a mid-level manager in an information services division, often had something worthwhile to say, but instead of opening his mouth, he usually got into a silent argument inside his own head. "Damn it! They are way off base. Don't they see what they are missing?" Bob gets more agitated and ends up talking to himself in a negative loop.

To himself he said, "Why don't you speak up?"

And he answers to himself, "Well, I don't want to look like I'm a know-it-all. Besides, what if I'm wrong? I will look like an idiot. The last time I piped up, people were snickering, and the boss kept staring at his watch."

"So now you are just going to sit here and be silent?"

"I have to work with them every day. I'm not going to act the fool."

No wonder Bob was so quiet in meetings. That noisy internal commentary kept him totally preoccupied! By the time he mustered up enough courage to speak, the meeting had moved on to another subject. Stuck in a degenerative negative loop, Bob silently chastised himself for missing "another opportunity to weigh in."

Silence is not a passive act. Bob was not just sitting there. He was very busy hiding what he was really thinking and feeling. It takes a lot of energy to actively keep your mouth shut. "Withholding Silence" covers up self-consciousness that comes from fear. When you withhold, you are assuming negative intentions, and putting yourself in a Victim attitude. You are missing everything in which you want to engage because your attention is focused only on yourself. When you are not paying attention to the external world, you miss out. No real action can take place when you are in a state of Withholding Silence.

The Cost Of Withholding Silence

The degenerative mindsets that lead to the Withholding Silence do not go away by themselves. You have to intentionally confront them and replace them with generative mindsets. This requires a deep honesty and willingness to be uncomfortable. The discomfort comes from facing how much the degenerative loop is costing you on a personal and professional level.

Bob decided to hire a coach to help him change these detrimental patterns at a root level. He confronted his own reticence to make public mistakes by admitting his years of withholding silence were more problematic to his career than any mistakes he could have made by speaking out.

> Coach: "Bob, what is your fear or concern about engaging in dialogue?"
>
> Bob: "Well, first off, I am worried that if my ideas are not thought through, I will look like a complete idiot. Or it may look like I am grandstanding, just speaking to look good in front of my boss."
>
> Coach: "That is a great double bind. Let's take the first one, looking like an idiot. How does that happen?"
>
> Bob: "For instance, in yesterday's meeting, I had a hunch that they were going down the wrong path, but I didn't know why. It took me a few minutes to realize the why, but then it seemed too late."
>
> Coach: "What do you mean 'too late'?"

Bob: "They had moved on to another part of the project."

Coach: "So, let's look at the cost of your silence. What does it cost the project if they do not include your hunch?"

Bob: "About a week's worth of work. Not only that, the team will be de-motivated because it will seem like a redo."

Coach: "How about for you, personally?"

Bob: "Well, I beat myself up over not speaking, and then I am de-motivated and tune out completely."

Coach: "When you tune out, how does that impact your peers, your boss?"

Bob: "I'm sure I bring the whole energy level down a few notches. When someone else checks out, I notice it. I am sure my boss is beginning to wonder if she made the right decision to bring me on to this leadership team."

Coach: "So, it sounds like your silence has a pretty high price tag."

Bob: "I sure hadn't thought about it that way, but yes, it does. What can I do?"

Coach: "What do you want to do?"

Bob: "I want to engage in a way that adds value."

Coach: "First, you need to be honest with yourself. When you don't speak, you are NOT adding value."

Bob: "Right. Ouch. I never thought of it that way."

Coach: "You are shooting yourself in the foot. Next, you need to ask yourself some questions. Before you open your mouth, ask yourself:

1. Do I want to say something just to look good?

2. Am I just repeating what has been said just to say something?

If the answer is "yes," keep your mouth shut, or you could engage by saying something like, "I have nothing new to add, but I agree/disagree with..." If the answer is "no" to number 1 and 2, it's time to show up. Ask yourself more questions:

1. How is what I have to say contributing to the discussion?

2. Am I disagreeing? If so, with what specifically?

Break it down so that when you do disagree you will be on target. If you have an objection but don't know exactly why, you can say, "I have a hunch that we are missing something here and I need a few minutes to think on it." Another option is to use qualifiers such as "This is off the top of my head..." or "My first thoughts are..." or "This is not fully baked..." You can add your own comments without committing them to be fully thought out."

Bob: "This is gonna be a stretch, but I'm willing to give it a try."

There is really no justifiable excuse for Withholding Silence. Bob eventually discovered that many of his so-called half-baked ideas actually stimulated valuable discussions and his contribution was greatly appreciated.

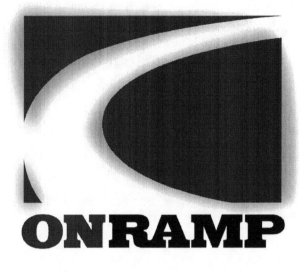

ENGAGEMENT ON-RAMPS

Sometimes you can help others give up their withholding patterns by enforcing a simple communication technique that makes a real difference without much confrontation. Hanna, a marketing vice president, decided to track who was engaging in her team discussions and who was not. "I would like to hear from the people who have not spoken." Then she would go around the room and ask each person on her list to share their thoughts. "What do you feel about this proposal? What are we missing? Where are you in agreement? Do you disagree?" Hanna's questions provided a context for everyone to speak up, and her specific questions gave people tangible ways to engage. After a few sessions, most of Hanna's team learned the routine and volunteered comments rather than needing to be singled out and asked.

The Silence Of Compliance

Ben, a director, presented his proposal to his team and then asked, "What do you think of my idea?"

"Sounds OK," one member responded with a bit of hesitation.

"It should work," another chimed with a question mark at the end of the sentence.

"I have no objections," the third member half-heartily commented.

Ben noticed the lackluster responses, but thought to himself, "It's the end of the day and they must be tired." The meeting was over.

Over the next few weeks, Ben was puzzled when his team failed to execute the plan they had seemingly approved. He spent hours trying to get things moving, never realizing that the root cause of the problem was his own leadership. He had never led his team to an official agreement in the first place! The unvoiced objections of his team were expressed in covert resistance. This is called the "Silence of Compliance." When people nod their heads without speaking up, you can bet they are either not paying attention or they are disagreeing. Obviously, the Silence of Compliance is not passive and speaks volumes, usually too late.

What are Ben's options? If he is willing to be present, tell the truth, and engage his team in a two-way conversation, he can pierce the silence and make some real changes. His opening lines might be, "OK, I am underwhelmed by your lack of enthusiasm for my proposal. I want to hear what you really think. Listen, I am not looking for agreement. I want your honest feedback."

Team Player A: "All right. Ben, this plan seems like a lot of work with no value added."

Ben: "Well, you are right about short-term impact. What do you think about the long term? I believe there will be long-term value and it's worth the effort."

Team Player B: "I know my people will be put off by this because they'll figure it's just another flavor-of-the-month idea that is being pushed on them again."

Ben: "Truth is, I'd like to understand how they feel about the proposal. Then I'd like to ask them what they need from me in order for them to get behind this."

Team Player C: "I have no objections, but I'm afraid of what I'll hear. What should I do to handle their potential resistance?"

Ben: "I respect these people and it's important we get them involved from the bottom up. I understand your trepidation, but how about inviting them to talk about what they want and then get it down on paper? And I'm open to compromise."

Ben was able to open up the space to create a two-way, maybe even a ten-way, street. He invited his team to engage in his leadership decisions, broke through his own silent compliance, and cut to the truth of what his people were really thinking.

Intentional Silence — A Powerful Communication Tool

"Intentional Silence" is a conscious choice to not speak until the time is right. It only can happen when you are present, calm, and focused. You are paying full attention to the person or group you are talking with by watching, listening, and feeling how they are responding to your communication. An example of Intentional Silence is when you ask a tough question and let the person sit and perhaps even squirm without speaking or trying to rescue him.

The rescuer in you will want to remove the discomfort of confrontation, but this is not the time to be a hero. Do not chastise yourself for being mean or cruel. Intentional Silence is not a critical silence. It comes from recognizing that whomever you are communicating with is fully capable of expressing himself and deserves to have the chance to speak his truth. When you jump in rather than letting the person work or even struggle a little with a provocative question, you actually rob him of a valuable process that usually helps him grow stronger.

Markus, a marketing executive, wants to get promoted. The culture inside of his division consists of verbally engaging people who eagerly "toss the meat on the table and chew on it." They can become very loud and sometimes may appear to be aggressive with each other but will usually walk away from the table with a sound decision. Markus, an introvert by nature, has received feedback from his boss that he is not weighing in at the meetings. Markus is reticent to engage in banter at that level and has many judgments and criticisms about his colleagues. In fact, he has said, "I would never do what John does. He just throws ideas out there without thinking them through."

When Markus originally filled out his personal values statement, he listed "honoring diversity" as one of his core values. It became apparent to his boss and mentor he was not applying his value of diversity to the vigorous talkers in his division. His mentor confronted him with this contradiction.

The Mentor: "Honoring diversity is very important to you?"

Markus replied, "Very."

Mentor: "I don't understand then. You want to honor differences but do not honor the type of person who you claim is verbally aggressive. Do your values only apply when they fit into your picture of how you think people should be?" His mentor just sat there and looked at him while Markus sat there stewing.

After a few moments, Markus turned bright red and asked, "Why are you doing this to me?"

His mentor, unperturbed, kept eye contact and quietly responded, "You haven't answered my question."

Markus blurted out, "Go away." His mentor calmly and firmly said, "Just as soon as you answer my question."

A long Intentional Silence filled the room.

Markus finally shifted gears, softened, and said, "OK...I got it. I don't like it, but I got it."

Intentional Silence is a powerful tool. It allows you to have a positive confrontation, point out an important issue, and hold the silence to create the space for the solution or resolution to come about. Intentional Silence allows you to hold your ground confidently because you know you are there for another person's success and you will not let him off the hook to be anything less than his full potential. By the way, Markus's story has a happy ending. About two months later, Markus was fully engaged in conversations with his team and received a positive performance rating on his next review.

Cafeteria Rescue

Sean asked tough questions, but within moments of asking, he would do the "Cafeteria Rescue" by offering a menu of possible responses.

Sean: "So Tony, what are you going to do about this tricky situation?"

Tony thinks about the question, visibly uncomfortable.

Almost immediately Sean says, "Maybe you could write a list of all the alternatives and circle the top three? Maybe you could have your team come up with a solution or..." Sean would rattle on as if he were brainstorming with Tony rather than letting Tony grapple to discover his own answers. Most of us have the urge to toss ideas out there like life preservers to save the person rather than letting him swim on his own. Intentional Silence is a skill that takes practice to develop, but it brings people into a place where they can be creative.

As we have acknowledged several times now, another example of Intentional Silence occurs when you consciously choose that speaking up about a thought, perception, or feeling of yours would truly not serve the best intentions of yourself or the other person. This can be a very subtle decision and requires reflection and self-honesty, as well as being open to feedback from others. For example, we often run into situations on teams in which one team member feels disliked or rejected by another. We might hear a team member say, "I've tried to be her friend in so many different ways, but she just doesn't seem to want to talk to me." There can be many causes of such situations, of course, and a Real Conversation can help explore and sometimes resolve them. And sometimes, what we discover is that the other person — whether it be a colleague, a supervisor, a direct report — is not interested in or open to the same objectives or interests. In this case, for example, not everyone wants to have "friend relationships" at work. This is different from the category of business issues where your point of view might be controversial. In those cases where it is on the personal side of things versus work related, it may be best, or at least more strategic, to choose to not pursue personal objectives or discussions with that person at work. To hold silence on those issues at work, or find a more appropriate time such as after hours or another outlet for them, might be a better choice. Making that type of decision can sometimes bring a very real sense of peace or satisfaction, as well.

"Silence is one of the great arts of conversation."
Marcus Tullius Cicero

We're Not Gossiping. We're Networking.

DEALING WITH GOSSIP

Gossip is when you talk negatively about somebody else behind his or her back. Conspiring against others is a more lethal form of gossip, is non-productive, and often hugely detrimental. If you find yourself saying, "Stay away from that person, they are really bad news," STOP, keep your mouth shut, and ask yourself, "What is my motivation for this kind of negative talk? What does it take for me to have a Real Conversation with that person directly rather than blabbing to someone else?" These situations beg for silence and introspection.

Being the recipient of gossip is also a problem. Sandra was a good listener. Many people came to her office to talk, often negatively, about co-workers. She supported these exchanges with nonverbal encouragers by nodding her head and acting interested, with an occasional "uh-huh." Everyone felt better after dumping in her office, but would often return a week later with the same complaints about the same person. Sandra praised herself for being such a good listener, but eventually felt she was being used and participating in being used as well. To herself she would say, "Why do I allow these people to spew their problems all over my office week after week? It certainly does not help anyone. I'm tired of all this."

Sandra felt trapped. She realized she was playing both the victim and the rescuer. She needed to shift gears and begin to confidently tell everyone to talk directly with the person they had the issue with rather than come to her. But she worried if she confronted anyone, she'd lose her "friends."

The truth is listening to gossip is just as bad as talking gossip. The silence of listening gives nonverbal approval and supports the person to continue instead of taking clear action to change a problem or simply let it go. It took some coaching, but Sandra eventually learned how to stop inviting in the gossipers in. She moved into the coach role and began to ask, "How can I support this person to take care of this issue himself? How can I empower him instead of feeding this poison?"

Martha, a director of operations, interrupted people, often in mid-sentence, when they were gossiping. "Hold on here. Have you had this conversation with Ted?" If the person said no, she'd insist, "Let's get Ted on the phone because I'm sure he would like to hear this directly from you." If the person refused, she'd ask, "What is stopping you from going to Ted with this issue?" and coach him or her to identify reservations. Martha held her people accountable and nudged them along. "When will you have the conversation? Let me know how it goes, and soon." This practice helped eliminate gossip in her organization because Martha was clear and simply would not tolerate it.

CONSIDER THIS:

1. What are two ways you can engage in conversations when you have something important to say, but may be intimidated to speak up?

2. Do you gossip about others? Listen to gossip? When will you approach those you have been gossiping about and have Real Conversations? How can you coach those who are gossiping to have Real Conversations?

3. Think of how you could use silence intentionally to reinforce your message.

> *"If you talk to a man in a language he understands,*
> *that goes to his head. If you talk to him in his language,*
> *that goes to his heart."*
> **—Nelson Mandela**

BEST PRACTICES
FOR REAL CONVERSATIONS

You cannot script a Real Conversation, but you can prepare for them by thinking about three things: 1. What is the outcome that you want? What actions, results do you want to see happen? 2. What do you want the other person to experience during and after they talk with you? Following are best practices for having Real Conversations. Add them to your conversation tool box.

1. HAVE YOUR OPENING LINES READY

While there is no way to know exactly what you will encounter on the freeway, negotiating the on-ramp is critical to getting to your destination. Having your opening lines ready gives you a strong entry point and the confidence to handle any hesitation you may feel. Once you have spoken your opening lines, you are in the conversation and there is no turning back. This is a good thing. Your opening lines help put you in a frame of mind that reminds you and the other(s) of your positive intent.

For example, you can open with, "I would like to have a conversation with you about how we work together and how we can improve our communication," "Let's get on the same page," or "There are some issues I think we really need to discuss and get on the table so we can find some solutions." Stating your positive intent for the conversation sets the tone so that this is not a dumping or blaming session, but rather a chance to really make a connection and a difference.

Tony would regularly create an entire outline of his Real Conversation prior to having it. His practice helped guide him through, and if he got stuck he would use his notes to make sure he didn't leave anything out. His key points always gave him a sense of confidence and pulled him through the emotional swells that would often arise.

Sample Opening Lines

Here are four different categories of opening lines that deal with:

1. Performance issues

2. Raising organizational issues

3. Opening questions if you are in a leadership position

4. Openers for Real Conversations with peers and colleagues

Openers For Performance Issues

The following four examples are listed in order of intensity, from the least intense (more question-based) to the most intense (more directive). Take these examples and make your own version of them so that you can say them in a way that is natural.

1. "In general, how is work going for you? How is it for you being on this team? How do you think you are performing? What would enhance your performance? How can I support you better as your boss? What are your thoughts about _____ aspect of your work?"

You can see by this first example you are asking questions, wanting to engage the person in opening up, and encouraging her to talk about her perceptions and from where you are coming.

2. "There are some issues regarding how you work or the results of how you are producing that need to change. I would like to discuss each of our perceptions and then together create a plan that will close the gap... If you could change one thing to improve how you work, what would it be?"

In this instance you are more directive. You are pointing to some more specifics, and you are stressing the aspect of partnership.

3. "During the past _____ (weeks or months — I left out years intentionally), I have noticed a marked change in your _____ (performance, behavior, or impact on others). I would like to hear what your perceptions are and discuss what my perceptions are and then come up with some action plan that we can put into place."

In this case, you are really being more specific about what you are talking about and, again, you are inviting her to comment before you do.

4. "Over the past _____ (weeks or months), I have noticed an increasing gap between where I think you can perform and where I see you are performing. I am bringing this to your attention now because we are at a threshold where it is a priority, and changes need to be made. I would like to

explain what I have been noticing and then hear how you see your performance and where you think you can close the gap."

In this fourth example, you are even more direct, more to the point, more specific. You are actually putting it into her hands regarding what to do.

Opening Lines For Organizational Issues

These statements and their complementary questions can be customized and used when putting organizational issues on the table. They are listed from the mildest to the most intense.

1. "An opportunity that we are missing is…"

2. "What are the opportunities that we are missing?"

This opener shifts the frame from mistakes to opportunities.

3. "A pattern that I have been noticing is…"

4. "What are the patterns that you have been noticing?"

By speaking from the first person, you take full responsibility for what you perceive and reduce the likelihood that others will think you are blaming them.

1. "A process that we need to re-examine or reevaluate is…"

2. "What process do we need to re-examine or reevaluate?"

You are pointing to something more specific and directing the activity toward solutions.

3. "One area where we can improve is..."

4. "What is one area where we can improve?"

You are moving toward a solution in this statement, and you have an idea of how things can be better.

5. "This is an area where we need to be working more closely together..."

6. "Where do you think we need to be working more closely together?"

You are making a specific focus and moving toward the result of working together, focusing on positive intent as the result.

7. "One place where we shoot ourselves in the foot is..."

8. "Where do you suppose we are shooting ourselves in the foot?"

This is a way that you can point out to the group how behaviors are really not very effective without pointing blame at someone in particular.

9. "Something that we have been doing for ____ (weeks or months) that no longer makes sense to me is..."

10. "What have we been doing that no longer makes sense?"

This is a good one for processes that are already in place, but now you realize it is time to rethink it, and again, without laying blame on anyone. Often external situations change or there is new information that needs to be considered.

11. "A question that we have not asked yet is..."

12. "What is the question that we have not asked yet?"

People like questions because it allows them to come up with answers. This opener makes a space for discussing the issue.

13. "Something that we seem to avoid discussing is..."

14. "What does it seem like we avoid discussing?"

This opener is more provocative and will get people's attention.

15. "There is an issue that needs to be put on the table."

16. "What is the issue the needs to be put on the table?"

These are openers that are direct and to the point.

17. "As leaders, there is something we are not hearing."

18. "What is it that we are unwilling to hear?"

This opener raises the ante for the whole leadership team.

19. "One topic that we simply seem unwilling to engage in is..."

This is another opener that will get immediate attention.

The last openers bring a sense of urgency to the issue:

20. "An accident that is waiting to happen is..."

21. "We cannot afford to continue..."

22. "Something that we urgently need to address is..."

Opening Questions For Leaders

The questions in the third group are great openers for organizational issues. Leaders find these useful when they are walking around the office for input or are making a site visit to a business unit.

1. "What changes have you noticed taking place?"

2. "What have been the tough issues that you are dealing with?"

3. "What would you say the state of the morale is? What is the hallway talk?"

4. "What is something that you want to ask, but hesitate to ask?"

5. "What is a process that you think we need to change?"

6. "What change would make the biggest impact on the company? For your division? For you personally?"

7. "What do you see from your perspective that may be an issue of which the management team does not seem to be aware?"

This is a great question to help point out blind spots. Very often there is a separation between the line and management, and this is a way that you can invite valuable comments.

8. "What one change do you think our customers would like to see most?"

If you are in a central function, asking this of somebody that is in a particular branch, area, or function can really give you the best kind of pulse on what the customer is thinking.

9. "What one change in systems or equipment would make the biggest difference in our performance or in your performance?"

The people closer to the line are often more aware of what needs to be changed. Asking this question takes you to the heart of what is going on.

10. "If you could change one thing about how we do business, what would it be?"

When you ask people to freely tell you what their opinion is about something you share, you are guaranteed to be on your way to having a Real Conversation.

Opening Lines For Real Conversations With Peers And Colleagues

1. "One area in which I think we could do better is..."

2. "What is one area which we could work better together?"

3. "One thing I have noticed in the way we work together is..."

4. "One place that seems uncomfortable for me is when..."

5. "What is the one thing I could do to work smoother with you?"

6. "One recurring situation that I get frustrated with is..."

7. "What situation is causing friction in how we are working?"

8. "I am not sure what your thinking is around..."

9. "One place where it seems like we step on each other's toes is..."

10. "A pain-point in how we work is..."

11. "I do not understand what your intended impact is when you say..."

12. "What am I doing that does not make sense to you?"

13. "I do not understand what your intended impact is when you do..."

14. "One thing that I have a strong reaction to is..."

15. "What am I not noticing?"

What Are Some Opening Lines You Could Use?

"We cannot solve our problems with the same thinking
we used when we created them."
— **Albert Einstein**

2. FRAME AND STATE THE ISSUES

Let the person know with clear, recent, and relevant examples what the issues are, what needs to change, and
how you will know success has been achieved.

Jim begins his Real Conversation with, "I want to discuss
how you are getting your work done and how you might
improve your productivity." He follows with examples,
always working in threes. "Let me give you three examples of what it is that I'm talking about: One, it seems that
when orders come in you do not prioritize them; you treat
all of them as top priorities. This creates an overload. Two,
you are not closing out the orders right away, and that
is hurting your performance metrics. Three, it seems that

you take breaks during peak times rather than at times when the call flow is lower."

Now that the person knows exactly what is on the table, Jim continues with: "And here is how I think you can improve: One, you need to prioritize the calls according to the time urgency—which ones need immediate action and which ones can wait. Two, close out your orders as soon as they have been resolved. Do not wait until the end of your shift. Three, look at the call volume and be flexible as to when you have your breaks."

By framing the issues and letting others know what it is you are talking about, you create a context for an effective Real Conversation. Rather than just launching into a specific, you need to introduce the general category and then go into details.

Suggested Lines For Framing/ Stating The Issues

1. "The issue is..." "The issues are..."
    Give a current and clear example.

2. "Here is the background... This is how things have progressed."
    Give historical background in terms of how this issue has evolved.

3. "T he impact is..."
    Tell the person what the impact is and what it is costing the organization. Bring the urgency around the issue to the person's awareness.

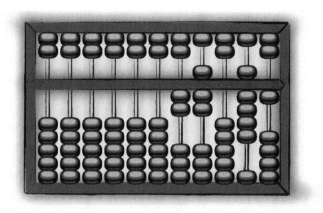

"Hold everybody accountable? Ridiculous!"
— **W. Edwards Deming**

3. BE FULLY ACCOUNTABLE

By taking full responsibility for what has happened, you model the behavior that you want the other person to assume. If you don't take full responsibility, you run the risk of falling into a blame frame and triggering a defensive response in others.

Fred took responsibility for the timing of his Real Conversation by saying, "An obvious question is, 'Why now?' I noticed these behaviors months ago, but I didn't say anything and I really should have at that time."

Greg addressed his new team of senior sales people who were not happy with his management style by saying, "I realize that my old way of leading wasn't the right way with this team. I know I have created a lot of distrust and dissatisfaction and I take full responsibility. And I apologize for how I have impacted any of you in a negative way." That statement elicited a big sigh of relief from the team. Within a few minutes a couple of his team members said, "I realize that I did not tell you how you were impacting me, so it's not all your responsibility." They stepped up an owned the situation because the leader did.

When you take full accountability and clean up (apologize when appropriate), it really opens up the space so that people can also step into full accountability. When you lay blame on someone, it usually makes her resistant to being accountable, and she falls into the natural knee-jerk response of being defensive.

Suggested Lines For Being Accountable

"I take full responsibility for what has happened."

"I own what has happened."

4. SET THE TABLE FOR FEEDBACK AT THE BEGINNING OF THE PROJECT

It is much better to be proactive about eliciting feedback than to wait. If you are working on a matrix team, as many people do, or a project team, the beginning of the project is the time to set up the norms for communication.

Fred was assigned the job of reorganizing four factories as project manager in Puerto Rico. On his first day, he sat down with each of his key business partners. Fred said, "This is how I like to work. I like to have open, honest, direct communication. When things are working, let me know. If something is not working, tell me as soon as possible. Take me aside and let me know what it is, and we can talk about it and work it out. I would much rather work that way than wait until something is way out of line."

The nice thing about what I call "setting the table" in this way is that it only takes a couple of minutes. A Real Conversation with real impact does not have to take a long time. All you need to do is be proactive and intentional about creating the context for these communications to take place, and then they can last as long as they need to last.

If you are a high performer and somebody comes to you with feedback, it is important to remember you may take it a lot harder than others. You may even want to punish yourself for making a mistake. But remember, whoever comes to you is showing up with positive intent. They may not be able to communicate what is going on in the best way. They may blame you. They may be emotional. The important thing is to assume that they have positive intent. They are bringing this information to you to support you to be better at what you do and at how you do it.

Mary, a middle manager at Pro Inc., was great at receiving feedback. She had an innate curiosity to understand what each person was trying to communicate. This helped her bypass any personal reaction to what was being said. Mary also liked to ask specific questions to delve deeper. "What do you mean by that?" "Can you give me an example?" "Tell me how that impacted you." "What is your thinking?" Since she was not defensive, she could indulge in this type of questioning like an empathetic scientist, eager to discover how she could improve. Mary never thought of herself as a failure or a victim, but always as a lucky executive who had the opportunity to up her game.

5. HANG IN WITH EMOTIONS

You want passionate people in your workplace. Passionate people come with a full set of emotions. Yet you may have reservations about engaging someone in a Real Conversation because you are afraid of their emotional reaction. People come to work with their emotions. If what you are talking about is important, more than likely there are emotions connected with it on both sides. Expect that people will have an emotional response in all Real Conversations.

Respecting another person's emotions creates the space for those emotions to take their rightful place as part of the landscape. They are not meant to make up the entire landscape, but nor should the landscape be devoid of emotions. Making room for emotion allows you to witness them without feeling you have to do something about them or cut them off. Your emotional intelligence (EI/EQ) will determine your ability to effectively deal with the emotional dimensions of any Real Conversation. The first use of the term "emotional intelligence" was in Wayne Payne's doctoral thesis, A Study of Emotion: Developing Emotional Intelligence from 1985. However, prior to this, the term "emotional intelligence" had appeared in Leuner (1966). Greenspan (1989) also put forward an EI model, followed by Salovey and Mayer (1990), and Daniel Goleman (1995.) The EI model contains four essential abilities: 1. Perceiving emotions — the ability to detect and decipher emotions. Perceiving emotions represents a basic aspect of emotional intelligence, as it makes all other processing of emotional information possible. 2. Using emotions — to facilitate various cognitive activities, such as thinking and problem solving. The emotionally intelligent person can capitalize fully upon his or her changing moods in order to best fit the task at hand. 3. Understanding emotions — the ability to comprehend emotion language and to appreciate complicated relationships among emotions. 4. Managing emotions — the ability to regulate emotions in both ourselves and in others, and manage them to achieve intended goals.

You may find that emotions make you feel overwhelmed, make you want to dismiss them, or make you want to save the other person from their emotions. Let us look at a few ways you can deal with emotions when they arise.

First, you need to understand the positive intention of emotions. There are three fundamental reasons that people get upset.

1. People get emotionally upset because there is a mismatch between what they perceive happening in reality and what they have in their minds.

2. People get upset because they care. If the issue were of trivial importance, they would not get upset.

3. People get upset when they perceive their values are being violated.

Identifying which reasons apply in a given situation gives you a perspective to engage the person in a positive way. The most difficult emotions for people to handle in a business context are disappointment, anger, and sadness. When you connect with the positive intention, emotions can be hugely informative. They signal that something important is happening. If someone is disappointed, angry, or sad, know that he is taking the topic seriously. People do not get upset if they do not care.

Give others a chance to have their emotional reactions. You do not need to do anything except acknowledge and respect what a person is feeling. The person may need a break, so you can offer a ten-minute time-out or to pick up the conversation another time that week.

Below is a table that lists the key emotions, their processes, their positive intentions, and how you can engage the person experiencing the emotion in a Real Conversation.

Emotion	Emotion— Process	Positive Intent	Engage them by...
Disappointment	He is let down by an expectation that is unfulfilled. Can lead to de-motivation if he sees a future of loss.	He has high expectations and is committed to results.	Acknowledge his expectations and lead to a new set of expectations.
Anger	A defense for the fear of losing something.	He knows what he wants. He has a lot of energy and focus. He has a sense of urgency.	Acknowledge the goal he wants to accomplish. Reassure him in your confidence in his ability to achieve.
Sadness	Grief over the loss of his goal.	This person puts his heart and soul into his work; he cares and is committed.	Be there, let him feel, then guide him to move to set new goals.

6. CULTIVATE EMOTIONAL VIGOR

Frank raised his hand in one of my seminars and said, "If the person cries on me, I'm toast. I'm lost. I don't know what to do." Frank needs to learn how to be present to emotions. That means that you are aware of what is going on for the person without having to "do" anything. In order to be present, you need to prepare yourself for emotion.

- The more comfortable you are with your own emotions, the more you can simply be with another person's expressed feelings.

- Learn how to accept being disliked by the person. She may not like to hear the news you have to tell her. Although she may not say it, she could have strong negative thoughts about working with you for a period of time. That is an acceptable part of the process. Leadership is not a popularity contest. Learn how to allow people to have their reactions and to be confident that you are taking the right action. Let them have their space.

- Some people will try to use their emotions intentionally or unintentionally to influence you by either intimidating you or attempting to make you feel bad in some way. You cannot lead an organization nor have a Real Conversation if you are always bending to people's emotional influence. The image of a massive boulder in the bottom of the ocean can help you stay grounded and calm in the midst of turbulent emotions.

- Preparation for dealing with emotionally charged situations will help you get a firm grip on your outcomes.

- Be an observer and pay attention to the other person's nonverbal behaviors (postures, expressions, gestures, tone of voice) as well as her words without getting swept away by their emotions. This observer's vantage point also allows you to articulate what you see. Rather than name a specific emotion, just leave it open-ended. "I can see this brings up a lot for you." "I can see that you have a lot of feelings about this issue." "I can see that this is really important to you." "I can see that this is bothering you because it's important to you."

- Do not say, "I can see that you are sad," or "I can see that you are angry." Instead, go with the positive intent of that emotion. "I can see that this is an important issue for you."

- Sometimes when emotions come up, you need to pause. You can say, "I can see that you are feeling a lot right now. Do you want to take a break? We can come back in five minutes" or "We can come back tomorrow." Give the person the option to compose themselves. They may say, "No. Let's continue on," or they may say, "Yes, I just want to take a ten-minute break," or "Let's get back to this tomorrow." Give them that emotional space.

Emotions are part of being human and you don't have to avoid or diminish them. Simply let emotions be emotions and they will take care of themselves.

7. ESTABLISH A PLAN

Every Real Conversation has tangible results. Set regular checkpoints to track those results over time. At the end of the conversation, articulate clearly what the plan is and what follow-up will look like. For most situations, the plan is collaboration between the two of you in which you are demonstrating your active support for the person. Do not have the conversation in January and then wait until June to have the next conversation. Best practice is to have follow-up conversations in regular intervals so that you are keeping tabs on things. Having regular checkpoints will help ensure success in implementing your plans. When he or she comes in for those checkpoints, ask:

- "How are you doing?"

- "What are your successes?"

- "Where do you need support?"

- "Do you think you are going to be able to make the deadline?"

- "Do you see yourself succeeding here?"

- "What do you see as your own prognosis?"

Also, acknowledge positive changes so that you really come from a place of encouragement. "These are the positive changes that I see happening."

Questions To Invite Developing A Plan

- "How do you think we should move forward?"

- "What will you do?"

- "How can I support you?"

- "When will we have a follow-up?"

- "What would follow-up look like?"

If you want to be more directive, you can say, "I think we should meet in two weeks (or appropriate time interval), and at that time I would like to hear how you are doing toward your goals."

8. CLOSE WITH ACKNOWLEDGMENT AND APPRECIATION

It is always important to close a Real Conversation with an acknowledgment. Come up with something that validates your time together. At the very minimum, thank them for engaging and dealing with the tough issues and for moving forward.

Close the conversation by outlining what just took place. What are the key points? What are the key takeaways? What are the next action steps? Verify that you are both on the same page. Have them write a summary and send it to you. State your confidence in that person so that they feel they can solve the problem.

Here are some compelling closes that acknowledge and appreciate your Real Conversation. They often include a summary.

1. "I really appreciate the quality of listening and the way that you responded to me. I feel very confident that we are closing this gap. I'm looking forward to next year. I am confident that when we have our performance review, you are going to have a much higher grading in these areas that we have talked about."

2. "We have covered a lot of ground today, and I want to thank you for how well you listened. We came up with some really good solutions. You addressed the issues in a straightforward manner, and I feel confident in your success."

3. "We have covered a lot of ground today, and I want to acknowledge how well you listened to what I had to say. You did not get defensive. You really took it as coaching, and that really made me feel comfortable in giving you feedback. I want you to know that I am 100 percent behind you, and I look forward to our next follow-up meeting."

4. "To wrap up, I would like to thank you for how well you listened. I think you had some really good ideas. You asked me some great questions and that really worked for me. It made it more of an exchange. I want our feedback to go on into the future as well. I'm glad that we can engage with one another and come up with productive outcomes. I am committed to your growth and I feel like you have made some definite, positive steps today in contributing to your own success."

5. "This has been the best conversation I think we have had in a long time. I felt like you listened, you asked great questions, and I was able to be open, honest, and direct with you. That really builds my confidence in you."

9. PLAY A COUPLE OF SCENARIOS IN YOUR MIND

In planning you want to ask yourself, "How do I think he is going to respond?"

1. "What is the best-case scenario?" Plan for the best. If he takes it well, how will that go?

2. "What is the worst-case scenario?" If he is going to blow up or have a meltdown, how would he melt down? And if he has that reaction, what is the reaction you might have, and how would you handle it?

3. Think through what questions or objections he might have.

4. Put yourself in his shoes and formulate your responses to his objections or questions.

5. Formulate how you want to be if he has an emotional reaction to what you say.

CONSIDER THIS:

1. How can you build more trust with your team? What stories can you share to let people know what makes you tick?

2. With whom at work do you have the greatest amount of Public Operating Space? What has contributed to that? How could you expand your Public Operating Space with others?

3. Who are three people you could request feedback from in the next week?

Let's make better mistakes tomorrow.

WORST PRACTICES FOR REAL CONVERSATIONS

Typically, you look to positive role models to inspire and structure your behaviors, yet it is also valuable to examine the wrong way to do things. The following five worst practices may seem like no-brainers, but amazingly, this list represents the most common problematic and undermining behaviors that my colleagues and I have had to deal with repeatedly over the last fifteen-plus years.

An outstanding consulting firm reviews worst practices as an agenda item at their annual consultants meetings. It is a laundry list of instances in which the consultants did the wrong thing, what happened, and how they turned the situation around. In addition to being an amusing part of the off-site, talking about these problematic practices provides others with sharp lessons and mistakes they will hopefully avoid.

Most of the time, worst practices are not intentional, but their impact is palpable and undeniable. They do not follow the hallmarks of having a Real Conversation: be present, tell the truth, and keep a two-way conversation. As you go through the list, think about your own variations on the theme so that you can build awareness and can catch yourself before you fall into a non-productive pattern. To have a Real Conversation you need to be fully accountable and recognize that your words, silence, actions, and inactions make all the difference in the world.

Here are some proven ways to crash your Real Conversations:

FIVE WORST PRACTICES

1. Don't show up

2. Avoid emotional content

3. Blame and be defensive

4. Be distracted, interrupt, and don't listen

5. Be vague

1. Don't Show Up

This is the epitome of not being present. Not showing up is the best way to guarantee that your Real Conversation doesn't work. Not showing up sends a clear message to that person or group that they are not important. The same is true of being late. To avoid sending this message, it is better to say, "I am sorry but I need to take care of another urgent matter right now. Let's reschedule our appointment..."

Terry, a CEO, had a reputation for being late to meetings. His staff began to form the perception that he did not respect their time. They started doing some math while they were waiting, counting the number of executives and staff people in the meeting room, multiplying that number by annual salaries, and figuring out how much Terry's delay was costing the company in dollars, not to mention the cost to morale. Terry was finally confronted. His response was an arrogant, "Well, I'm the CEO." This message clearly sent the signal that he thought he was above everyone else and that their time wasn't important. Trouble was ahead.

2. Avoid The Emotional Content

People come to work with their emotions. Jack, a vice president in Operations, treated people like things. He referred to them as "resources." He believed that "resources" just needed a clear set of instructions and that was that. Whenever an issue came up where people showed any emotion, he would quickly change the subject. On one occasion, someone started to cry and Jack walked out of the room. Clearly Jack had issues around emotions.

You cannot expect people to engage and care about their work if you do not give them the room to have their feelings. While you are not expected to be a therapist, giving space for people to get heated, disappointed, or sad as well as excited, joyful, and energized is a crucial part of leading in the workplace. Want to leverage the intellectual capital of your organization? Do not forget that those brains have hearts attached and hearts and minds both working together will maximize the person's ability to contribute.

3. Blame And Be Defensive

Overtly laying blame serves to create a defensive response in others: "That was your fault," or shifting blame, "I would have done it on time, but Frank did not get me what I needed," or "I did my part, but they let it fall through the cracks." Blaming sinks you deep into drama and creates defensiveness from others. Break through to positive intent and you will be well on your way to having a Real Conversation. Speak from the first person and learn how to say, "I was frustrated with how you responded," instead of pointing the finger with, "You frustrated me."

Steve crossed his arms and said, "It's not me who has the problem here." A defensive stance closes the possibility of having a two-way conversation. When you are defensive or adversarial your ears fall off (often you can see them on the floor). As an adversary, you don't have to listen to what the other person is saying because you think you are right and the other person is wrong.

There are three points you can use to check to see if you are being defensive:

1. You think the other person is wrong and you are right.

2. You are tense.

3. It is impossible for you to step into the other person's shoes and perceive the situation from his or her point of view.

What to do? Take a moment to pause, look for positive intent, and put your ears back on. Ask some open-ended questions so you can understand the other point of view, not just your own. The new response could be, "What is the overall goal we are trying to achieve?"

4. Be Distracted, Interrupt, Don't Listen

Susan literally jumped to answer her phone calls. Sometimes she would actually say to the person she was talking to, "Wait a minute. I need to take this." She'd gab away on the phone while the person she was supposedly having a critical conversation with sat there and whiled away the time, wondering why that call was more important.

Tom could not resist looking at his "Crackberry" every five minutes, regardless of where he was. Those who worked with Tom realized that they were second fiddle to his addictive digital life.

Go ahead and answer the phone or look at your palm device in the middle of a Real Conversation. It won't be real anymore because you won't be present. Yes, your plate is full, if not running over, but the paradox is that fifteen minutes of quality time is worth more than forty-five minutes of multitasked time. Give your focus to the person you are talking with, and that quality of time will pay off.

George could never let anyone finish a whole sentence. He would interrupt mid-sentence and say, "Got it." Or, he would insert his own version of how he thought the thought might end. George thought he was a good communicator, but it only took a few interruptions before you believed he was totally disinterested in anything you had to say.

Unless you are truly psychic, be patient, listen generously, and let people finish their sentences. If the other person starts to repeat themselves, then feed back what you have heard them say, and ask if there is anything else.

5. Be Vague

Neal said, "You know, the other day there were a couple of things that happened, and I'm sure that they really weren't your intention, but if you can work on them, I think we could be much more productive. OK?" Baffled, Fran retorted, "What are you talking about?"

Being vague dilutes your effectiveness. Prepare your key points. Jot them down and refer to your notes during the conversation so that you stay on track. Always give recent specific examples. This will also help deliver the message in a clear and concise way.

CONSIDER THIS:

1. In addition to the five worst practices, what others can you come up with? Which of the worst practices have you done? What did it cost the relationship?

2. How can you catch yourself and put in a best practice to replace your non-productive pattern? Which best practice would you begin with?

3. Think about people you work with who exhibit one of the five worst practices. Despite his external behavior, what do you suppose his positive intent would be? How might you approach him to have a Real Conversation? What suggestions or best practices would you recommend for him?

"If we did all the things we are capable of,
we would literally astound ourselves."
— Thomas A. Edison

Part 3: Being Real

This section consists of real-life stories that bring to life the concepts that are presented in this book, how somebody transforms their thinking and mindset from unreal to real, and the conversations that result. You'll see how you can turn unproductive conversations and meetings into valuable ones that move things forward.

Part 3: Being Real

1. Where Are We going?
2. Getting to the Brutal Facts
3. Creating Clear Expectations
4. Ongoing Engagement
5. Feedback styles and best practices
6. Feedback Trilogy
7. Walk-n-Talk
8. Coaching for Professional Development
9. Coaching for Performance Improvement
10. Real Conversations with Your Peers
11. Real Conversations with Your Boss
12. A Case of Unclear Roles and Responsibilities

"It is the direction and not the magnitude which is to be taken into consideration."
Thomas Paine

WHERE ARE WE GOING?

O ne of the most important challenges for a leader is to strategize, craft, and communicate a vision for their organization. Setting the direction is meaningless unless you actively engage your people in Real Conversations that include asking and answering, "What is the Vision? Where are we going?"

So many talented business minds craft impeccable directives, but they fail to adequately translate what's on paper into the hearts, minds, and calendars of their people. Simply posting your vision on your intranet website will not cut it. No matter how much thought or time you spend putting your vision together, you will come up short if you cannot successfully communicate it and, more importantly, enroll the troops to align with it in theory and practice. Investing time and money to go off-site to build a vision does not guarantee your organization will engage with the vision; it has to be spoken into existence by you and your leadership team.

The Real Conversation — *"What is the vision? Where are we going?"* — is somewhat different from the other Real Conversations in this section. First of all, the CEO or department leader almost always initiates these conversations. They are usually launched at meetings with visual aids, and once the leader presents the vision, it is necessary to actively break into more intimate groups or one-on-ones to go deeper. Although this chapter does not focus on specific methods for writing a vision plan, it does address how to effectively engage your organization once you have the concepts, talking points, slides, or presentation in hand. You will also learn practical tips and tools to make your vision really inspire, inform, and catalyze more Real Conversations to take place.

THANK YOU, I CAN READ
THE SLIDES MYSELF

Tom, a senior executive, opened the January all-hands meeting of his division with his first slide. It featured the vision statement in bold type: "Our vision is..." Tom proceeded to read each and every one of the thirty-five slides in his presentation without taking a break! Most of his audience was in a deep all-hands trance by slide number three! About what percentage of his staff do you think could remember the key elements of the vision? You are right, next to none!

Tom failed to realize most people in his audience could read. Slides are merely a backup to your presentation. You do not need to read your slides nor pretend that by having great visual aids and pressing a clicker your organization will suddenly wake up and embrace your talking points. Remember, your audience follows your lead on all levels. Instead of being a robot, you need to be a real person. You are the main event. People are there to be led by you, not by a PowerPoint deck. If you want to initiate a Real Conversation that asks, "Where are we going?" and "What is our direction?" you need to be present, tell the truth about your enthusiasm, passion, and commitment, and engage your audience in the process. Your slides are there to focus the attention on what you have to say, period.

START WITH THE POSITIVES

To start her all-hands meeting, Sherry stepped in front of the podium with just the title slide on the screen. "Before I get into a discussion with you about the new direction for our division, I want to thank all of you for the incredible year we just had, filled with so many major accomplishments."

Sherry cordially invited her people to feel welcome. She then listed the teams responsible for each success and continued, "I want to acknowledge those of you who participated in the vision focus groups in August. The leadership team spent three days in late September integrating your valuable input as we crafted the direction for this upcoming year. With your help, we came up with a new focus that will certainly leverage our strengths and allow us to become more efficient and even more productive.

"I also want to take a few minutes and tell you how I believe our new direction will make a difference for me in my role as leader. And I want to share with you some of the concerns that keep me up at night so that we can use our collective brainpower to look at how we will meet the challenges before us. I look forward to hearing your thoughts when I finish my presentation."

Sherry was fully present, told the truth, and engaged her audience on a personal level. Her Real Conversation, "What is the vision? Where are we going?" inspired her entire staff. They totally enrolled, were eager to hear more, and enthusiastically gave her their best feedback.

ENGAGE THEM IN YOUR TOPIC

Sherry proactively focused her people during the presentation. "As I go through this deck of slides," she told them, "I want you to watch for three things: What is new? What will be different about how you work? What is unclear or what might you have questions about?"

Sherry read the vision statement and then immediately followed with, "This is what this statement means to me and the difference I see in how we will work." She went on to explain what the vision statement meant and then asked, "What does this vision statement mean to you? I really want to hear what you have to say. Take two minutes and talk to the person next to you and tell them what you heard. Then explain what the vision statement means to you, how your work will be different, and what questions you might have." After her people talked to one another, she invited questions.

Sherry fielded a few responses from the audience and then went on to discuss the strategic focus areas, how they were created, and how they made a significant difference in the operations of the organization. She also offered concrete examples of current projects and then asked, "How do you imagine your work changing now that we've taken a new direction?"

Again, her people took two minutes to talk with the person next to them. Sherry followed this pattern of mini-presentation/dyad throughout the three-hour period. In her closing remarks, she added, "I'd like each of you to write a statement describing what you heard today and include one question that you want to discuss in your next team meeting." She created a compelling experience for her audience by telling her story and having them engage in conversation at regular intervals during her presentation. After the meeting, people were buzzing with excitement. They felt they had a clear understanding of the vision and support for follow-up discussions.

When people are invited to make comments and formulate their questions in a safe environment, it helps them integrate the message. Giving them intervals to talk about what they have heard also helps them metabolize the concepts and surface the questions that would normally distract them from paying attention. It can be very intimidating to ask a difficult question when you are in a large group. But if you pair people up and encourage them to ask questions of one another, it really opens up a flow of interest, curiosity, and enthusiasm. The leader can then ask the whole group, "What were some of the questions or comments that came up in your discussions?" and since the question is presented anonymously, no one person is on the hot seat. This is a great example of supporting the two-way street required for a Real Conversation inside of a larger group setting.

ASK THE TOUGH QUESTIONS TO MAKE IT REAL

Here are some specific questions to further engage your people in The Real Conversation:

- "What is the vision?"
- "Where are we going?"

Expect that people will speak up when you invite them to give you their honest opinions. Make sure you are ready to hear and respond to their questions in a non-defensive way. If you respond from defensiveness, you will shut down any possibility of having a Real Conversation. If you shut someone down in public, then you are communicating to the rest of the people that it is not safe to speak up. Unfortunately, you will then get the Silence of Compliance, and you are stuck in a stalemate. When people do not get the opportunity to work through their doubts and objections and express them openly, they withdraw and will not be able to be a strong advocate for the vision.

At the end of your presentation, present your people with a follow-up list of questions (below). Ask them to honestly consider and answer the questions without fear of retribution. Then invite them to set up private Real Conversations in person if they feel they wish to share.

Follow-Up Questions

1. "What is your gut reaction to this vision?"

2. "What are the challenges you might have in moving this new direction forward?"

3. "What are you comfortable with/uncomfortable with?"

4. "How might elements of this vision not work or not be applicable to you?"

5. "Look into the future. Where do you imagine we might run into problems?"

6. "What will be the water-cooler talk about this new plan?"

7. "Any other suggestions or insights?"

ONE MEETING IS NOT ENOUGH

One mistake that leaders and leadership teams make is that they think that just one meeting is enough to get their message across. "I went over it in the all-hands meeting. Why are they still unclear? Don't they get it?" The answer is, not yet. Do not forget that others down in your organization have not had the exposure that you and your leadership team have had with the vision and/or strategy. While your vision may be clear to you, your entire staff may not understand all of it; certainly, they will have questions and/or may disagree with various points. Some people hesitate to raise their real issues because they are intimidated by the group size or the composition of the group. These unspoken issues can be the seeds of discontent, confusion, and/or frustration that will lower morale and ultimately diminish productivity. Be prepared to give the message over and over. Do not be dismayed when you hear the same questions repeated. This means it is time for some more Real Conversations.

To make sure everyone gets it, ask yourself, "How can I make it real and relevant for people?" Look at the vision/strategy from their point of view. Ask yourself, "What do I need to change in how and what I communicate to make it really stick?" It may be that aspects of the vision that were clear when you first presented it may need further explanation and/or interpretation as issues and challenges arise. Remember, each time you present the vision is another opportunity to inject your organization with enthusiasm and motivation.

Shirley was making an initial presentation to her leadership team on a vision she had been crafting. When she opened the questioning up, several of her direct reports queried, "Why are you including such a complex new set of metrics as part of the vision?" Shirley misinterpreted the question as a form of insubordination and resistance. Consequently, she responded with a sharp, "Maybe I was not clear. We ARE going forward with the metrics." Inside the minds of her senior team, people heard a sharp, "Don't ask any more questions, just shut up and do it!" Demotivated by her tone, her team shut down and refused to discuss the issue further. When it came time for them to roll out the vision to their staff, they had difficulty explaining the rationale for the stringent new metrics. As you can imagine, the metrics program had difficulty getting off the ground.

Shirley failed to present and respond with positive intent. She could have thought to herself, "Hmm. It sounds like they need some other kind of information, something I failed to share in my presentation." She could have responded to the question with, "What is the intention of your question?" She could have realized that her team wanted to know more so that they could better represent the initiative in order to field questions from their teams. Assuming positive intent means that you are listening from a point of view that allows for more information. In this way, you assume total responsibility for the communication and are present to respond rather than to react. It can make all the difference to the situation.

FIELD TOUGH QUESTIONS AND COMMENTS ABOUT YOUR VISION

Let's take a look at a few examples of questions you might ask and how to handle the comments from your people. Again, the key is to always assume positive intent. How you hear and respond to people's responses will determine if you are creating the opening for a Real Conversation to take place or shutting down the possibilities altogether. It is up to you.

Take One (with Negative Intent):

You ask, "What are the challenges that you see you will have in moving this plan forward?"

The response: "This will never work."

You respond, "The leadership team came up with this plan, and we are going forward with it."

Debrief: This is a defensive response that ignores the comments of the person who made the statement.

Take Two (With Positive Intent):

You ask, "What are the challenges that you see you will have in moving this plan forward?"

The response: "This will never work."

You respond, "What part of it do you think will be problematic?" or "What leads you to that conclusion?"

Debrief: This response acknowledges the comment and requests more specific information. This allows the person who made the comment to look for the specifics of what is missing for them rather than to generalize and dismiss the whole plan.

When people's objections contain the words "never" or "always," they are generalizing. In other words, they are taking one or two instances and making them into global assumptions. This is not useful. Your response, as a leader in any fashion, needs to give guidance to help others break down the generalizations into specific workable components.

Take One (With Negative Intent):

You ask, "What will be the water-cooler talk about this plan?"

The response: "This plan is pie-in-the-sky and the flavor-of-the-month."

You respond, "I don't agree with that statement. It seems that people just don't understand."

Debrief: The response is making the comment wrong by shifting the problem to the people around the water cooler.

Take Two (With Positive Intent):

You ask, "What will be the water cooler talk about this plan?"

The response: "This plan is pie-in-the-sky and the flavor-of-the-month."

You respond, "If that is what people are thinking, what do you think is needed to create a different, more positive response?"

Debrief: By directing people to focus on what is needed to create a positive response, you automatically lead them to a solution. Assume what they have been saying is true. As a leader, you have to manage perceptions. Take the perception as a starting point and ask the question that leads to a solution.

Take One (With Negative Intent):

You ask, "What is your gut reaction to this Vision?"

The response: "This plan is idealistic, not realistic."

You respond, "You obviously have not been listening to my presentation."

Debrief: This defensive response shuts down the comment by making it look like the person was not listening.

Take Two (With Positive Intent):

You ask, "What is your gut reaction to this vision?"

The response: "This plan is idealistic, not realistic."

You respond, "What was it you have been hearing that leads you to that conclusion?" or "What part of the plan sounds unrealistic?"

Debrief: By asking for qualitative information, you will gain a deeper understanding of what is missing for the listener.

Courtney, head of manufacturing, was comfortable fielding tough questions. "Our purpose today is to ask the challenging questions so the leadership team and I can noodle on them and come back to you with some solid answers." This gave the room permission to get tough and did not pressure the leadership to have an answer right on the spot. Of course, she was able to answer many concerns then and there, which gave her a sense of the change-readiness of her organization. When you ask the tough questions, you need to be ready to field the answers in a way that validates the person who asked.

FIVE TIPS TO GUARANTEE YOU SHARE YOUR VISION IN A REAL CONVERSATION

1. Be present

Your vision/strategy presentation needs to be a "gut grabber" for you and your audience. Sure it needs to inspire and motivate others, but how do you feel about it? When you think, talk, and present it, make sure the thoughts and ideas create a palpable feeling of enthusiasm and passion inside of you first! Your audience responds to your energy level and nonverbals far more than your words. If you are not vibrantly alive or fired up, your audience will feel like you do not care or might think that what you are saying is not that important. Remember, it needs to work for you first, but your vision needs to excite your leadership teams as well. When they go into the organization and communicate the message, they need to generate a real buzz.

Sometimes the passion behind a vision gets dissipated in copious amounts of language. Distill your text and come up with a couple of bullet points or one to three short phrases that express the vision in a nutshell without sacrificing the zest behind it. For example: "We bring data to life," "People, passion, purpose," or "People fall in love with our product." These become the "Hymn Sheet" that your team will use to encourage others to engage in the Real Conversation.

2. Tell the truth

Be open and vulnerable. Let people know your concerns. By being open and truthful, your organization can connect with you as a person and as a leader. Share yourself. For example, you might say, "The question that keeps me up at night is this: How are we going to increase productivity 30 percent? I know I cannot answer that question without all of you." Invite your organization to participate and make a personal connection, and you will shift the frame from, "Here is my vision. Follow me," to a very inclusive, "This is a problem we all need to get our heads around to be successful."

3. Engage your audience — It's a two-way street

Do not lecture. Every ten minutes or so break up your speech and engage in a dialogue with your audience. Encourage them to ask questions and jot down important ideas. Tell them you will answer their questions and that their feedback is crucial. Ask, "What have you heard me say?" "What specific questions or criticisms do you have?" Tell them, "I am going to get together with other leaders and come back with solid responses." Remember, you do not need to have all the answers right then and there.

4. Give them W.I.I.F.M.

Lofty, apple-pie vision statements can cause people to check out or worse. People want to know "What's in it for me?" (W.I.I.F.M.) Emphasize what will be different, new, and beneficial to people, not just the company. It is common for the audience to silently muse, "Oh, this is the same old vision as last year." Try to avoid the standard "... increase shareholder value..." line, and give everyone tangible examples of what will change and how it will make a positive difference up front and personal. Of course, you want to increase shareholder value, but you also want to personalize.

5. Communicate it in person

Bill and his leadership team spent three days off-site to craft their new vision and strategy. They came back and posted it on their intranet website and then followed with an email to everybody saying, "We have designed the vision for the year. Here is the link to the website."

How many people actually took the time to go to the website? That's right, next to none. Keep in mind that about 55 percent of the impact of your communication is in your body language, 38 percent in the tone of your voice, and about 7 percent in the specific words. Don't expect people to be thrilled about a one-dimensional PowerPoint on your intranet. They get the inspiration, motivation, and juice from a direct experience of you, face to face or at a meeting. Your passion brings the words to life and creates a vehicle that will transmit that intangible, yet palpable energy that will get the troops to do their best.

THINK OF YOUR PRESENTATION AS A THREE-LEGGED STOOL!

Melinda, a brand manager, delivered new project presentations that were long-winded and unfocused. "I need to tell them all of the details so that they can understand," she insisted. Truth be told, it is always better to tell others less and create a situation in which you engage people to ask questions. Remember, Real Conversations are a two-way street. Melinda's need to describe the texture of the bark on each tree in the proverbial forest blurs the salient points and keeps people disconnected from the information. Instead of telling them about the bark, Melinda needs to determine exactly what features she wants them to understand and, more importantly, remember.

Melinda needs to think of her talk as a three-legged stool. Imagine each of the key points of your talk as one of the three legs. People can easily hold three things in their mind. Take one of these points away and your talk will not hold any weight; it quickly topples. She decided she had to change her tune, so she implemented a process called "Chunking Up."

Melinda made a long list of points she needed to convey and then went through one by one and asked herself, "What am I really trying to say here?" She began to see major themes emerging, eventually ended up with about six themes, and proceeded to ask the same question, "What am I really trying to say here?"

Ultimately, Melinda narrowed down her presentation to just three key points. This exercise gave her newfound clarity. She no longer needed to prove herself and felt closer to telling the truth instead of padding her talk with excess data to impress. At the next presentation, her opening remarks were, "The three key themes I will cover today are what is new on the horizon, project updates, and concept review. As you listen to the first two topics, think about your ideas, feedback, and questions. I'll be asking you to get involved during the last theme, concept review."

Melinda opened up the floor for a two-way street and the staff was responsive and appreciative. After the meeting, two of her managers set up individual appointments for more in-depth Real Conversations.

A beefy appendix with all of the detail Melinda wants can be provided in follow-up slides and materials to convey her depth of knowledge.

BRING THE COMPANY VISION TO LIFE

Eric, a senior vice president of the engineering division of a large pharmaceutical company, is a strong believer in the company's new vision directive. One of his areas of responsibility is maintenance, both inside the laboratory and outside on the grounds. Eric makes a practice of walking the property and talking one-on-one with the many gardeners. He makes a point of telling them, "Because you are planting flowers and pruning trees, you are making the campus a very beautiful place. This helps create a wonderful environment for the scientists who are developing our medicines. When they walk these well-groomed paths, they feel a peaceful calm. So, too, do I. I just want to thank you for doing such a great job because you inspire them to do their best work."

By linking the gardeners' job of mowing the lawns to the job of scientists preparing compounds, Eric creates a powerful context for everyone in the organization to feel appreciated and connected. This act brings the company vision to life! And how long does it take? Maybe ten minutes! The return on this kind of investment of time and intention is enormous.

In order to have a Real Conversation, it is crucial to know to whom you are talking. When you are addressing someone from a smaller division of the company, it is especially important to find out what the person does and how they link to the bigger picture. Often people that are lower down in the organization are focused only on their daily tasks. They work hard, but they do not really have an opportunity to see how their particular contribution links to the vision of the company. Initiate a mini Real Conversation that acknowledges what they are doing and how it connects with the big picture. Make sure you invite them to give you feedback or ask you a question. Take time to listen and respond. These few minutes will not only energize whomever you are speaking with (often that type of motivation will last for months), but will also encourage them to consider having more Real Conversations on their own.

"One of the primary ways to de-motivate people is to ignore the brutal facts of reality."
—Jim Collins

GETTING TO THE
BRUTAL FACTS

One of the key elements identified by Jim Collins in his book, *Good to Great*, was that what great companies had in common was their ability to confront the most brutal facts of their current reality, act on their implications, and never lose faith.

Finding ways to speak about — and listen to — these "brutal facts" is a core element of Real Conversations. On the one hand, it takes courage to openly speak about issues that others may have strong reactions to. On the other hand, it takes another kind of courage to keep an open mind to the large range of interpretations that will inevitably come along with "brutal facts." And it takes even more courage to translate these conversations from a relationship or team to a whole company. Here is an example of a leadership team that we worked with to accomplish this.

Jack, CEO of a multi-national construction services company, was preparing to unveil a new vision for the company. The company norm for unveiling a vision was for the CEO to host a meeting with the senior team, go through a slick slide presentation, and then post the slides on the company website for everyone else to read. Jack really wanted to go beyond that: he wanted to make a major impression and create a step change in the organization with the new vision. He wanted to make the vision personal and to demonstrate to the company that the leadership was aligned to the vision.

To accomplish this, Jack's plan was to focus on the positives and strengths of the company. He brought this idea to the executive team, saying "I want to create a positive buzz about our new vision."

Brenda replied, "There is a lot of skepticism out there in the organization."

Jack's immediate response was, "Look I don't really care about a few nay-sayers. There is always going to be someone who is not happy."

Dean piped in, "It's not just a few people. Many people talk about the fear culture that is here."

"We don't have a fear culture here. We are all open," Jack quipped with an edge of irritation. The room went silent. All of a sudden Jack realized what had happened. His irate response had just killed the conversation in the room.

He looked at everyone and then said, "OK, I got it. Tell me more about what you have heard and what you have experienced." The whole room took a breath and a lively discussion ensued as more perspectives were shared almost at once:

"Several managers were fired on the spot by the last CEO after making critical comments about management in meetings that he was attending."

"If he didn't like what you said you were gone the next day. News of actions like that travels fast and very quickly many stopped talking in their meetings out of fear for their jobs."

Jack was having a hard time believing what he was hearing. He said, "That was then. I have never fired anyone because they spoke their mind."

"Yes, that is true but that is not what people remember," Brenda asserted. "All they remember is that the CEO fired people on the spot. It doesn't matter that you are the new CEO; the fear is still there."

Dean said, "If we want people to take this new vision seriously we have to get to the brutal facts."

"What is a brutal fact?" Jack asked.

"It's an unspoken or unacknowledged reality that stops people from moving forward. They all know that it's a fact but no one voices it," Dean explained.

"If we start talking about THAT it's just going to be a moaning and whining session that will go nowhere." Jack's voice was on edge again but this time he caught himself. "Wow, I can see how much I am resisting this whole idea of a fear culture and brutal facts. It just seems like we are going backwards rather than moving toward the future we want. My experience is that we just focus on what is wrong and never move forward as well as we could."

Carole spoke up. "If we don't address where we are today and what is really going on, we won't have credibility with the organization. This will just come across as another pie-in-the-sky flavor of the month. I don't want that. I want the people to sink their teeth into this new vision and feel like it's theirs." A wave of simultaneous head nodding went through the room.

Jack went on to say, "Well it seems like we all want the same thing. How can we get there?"

The team spent the next two hours talking about the steps they could take to demonstrate, all over the globe, that they were all personally aligned with and excited about the new vision, and to elicit that same kind of alignment and excitement from the rest of the company.

As they talked, they got even more excited, realizing that they had just experienced a step-change themselves. They had just succeeded at having a Real Conversation about topics — brutal facts — that had been looming but never before been voiced at the executive level. And they decided that they needed to have that same Real Conversation with the company as a whole.

Via town halls, video and satellite conferences, round table discussions, site visits, and teleconferences, the leadership team carried the new vision around the glove to the employees of their company. And in each conversation, they practiced this new discipline of naming the brutal facts. Each time, around the world, there were smiles and sighs of relief throughout the audiences when the leaders acknowledged the reality of the concerns and issues. Just as they had hoped when they committed to this process, they were gaining a high level of engagement and excitement by talking about the very things that they didn't really want to talk about!

It was during the Q & A sessions, however, that they really began to experience the power of what they were creating. In each session, each meeting, the questions came hard and fast. "Why isn't our pay equal to our competitors'?" "We've heard new visions before, how do we know you really mean this?" "Of course you'll take care of people in the main sites, but what about us out here in the smaller divisions?"

While many of the questions were tough and often unanticipated, Jack and his executive team responded appropriately and directly. They thanked each person who voiced a question and made sure to not diminish any of them — they wanted to model very clearly that the dialogue was open for the brutal facts, and that what they wanted in this new vision was for everyone in the company to work together on creating new answers.

In the wake of this series of meetings, there was a positive buzz throughout the company about the new vision. Of course, there were also many, many discussions about the concerns and brutal facts. But now these discussions were happening in the open, with motivation and hope to do something about them. Jack and his team had succeeded in opening up a company-wide Real Conversation that they were confident would now lead to coordinated action.

CONSIDER THIS:

1. Look at your vision statement. Does it pass the test? Does it excite you? Does your organization know what the vision is? What is in it for the people in your organization?

2. How have you communicated your vision?

3. What are three questions you could use to engage people in your vision?

4. What are the brutal truths that you have been unwilling to hear or deal with?

5. How do you stifle open conversations about what is not working?

"*Unhappiness is best defined as the difference
between our talents and our expectations.*"
— **Edward de Bono**

EXPECTATIONS INTO ACTION

According to a recent large research study by Career In-novations (www.careerinnovations.com), conversation gaps exist inside of all organizations. Their study revealed that most people want to have the Real Conversations that address "What's expected of me?" "How am I doing?" and "How will I be developed?" This chapter and the next give you the guidelines and practice to make sure you initiate these conversations and invite staff to participate on a regular basis.

In some businesses, employees receive a complete folder that lists their job description, roles, and responsibilities. Other organizations are not so thorough. "This is what your job is. Go figure it out." Depending on the type of person you are working with, the situation, and the complexity of their job function, the go-figure-it-out method can be very problematic. Creating clear roles and responsibilities allows people to clearly see what it is they need to do, and what they are going to be held accountable for as the year rolls on. It also opens the door for you to give feedback and helps them to be welcoming and responsive.

It is crucial that people know:

- Who is going to be doing what?

- What is the measurable output from each task?

- How will you know that the task is completed adequately? How will it be measured?

DECISION-MAKING

One of the first responsibilities you need to define is how decisions are made in your organization. Decision-making usually comes from the top down. The leader determines which decisions are his or hers and then considers various kinds of decision-making protocols that belong to the people below:

1. A decision made without input

2. A decision made with input

3. A decision made by consensus

4. A decision made by voting

5. A decision delegated to someone else

Each of these decisions can be elaborated depending upon which choices are being made. This kind of clarity sets up a fundamental basis for what people will expect and how they will interact and operate.

Some organizations run into big problems in decision-making. When potential scenarios are not clearly discussed beforehand, you will often hear a disgruntled, "Well, if Tom has this decision- making power and if Julie, on the team, is in strong disagreement, then she can request that the decision then be escalated." If the decision moves to the next level, what happens? Are you prepared to deal with the gray area? Make sure you create a variety of possible scenarios for multiple decision-making processes so that as you move forward, you know who does what, when, and why.

PROCESS FLOW—GETTING THE DELIVERABLES DOWN

Learn how to build a clear map of interdependencies. You will need to determine what level of detail you will need to get into as you are spelling out roles and responsibilities for a particular individual. In some cases, it is very salient to get to an extremely detailed level of explanation in terms of what a person needs to do. Some of the keys are:

- Making sure that the two of you are clear about what is expected

- How accomplishment will be measured

- When it will be measured

- How feedback will be given

As you set up this context at the beginning of a project or the beginning of your working relationship, check in on the progress at regular intervals.

During individual fifteen-minute Real Conversations, Rita would tell her people, "This is what I expect of you. You are going to have these five deliverables ready. They are due January fourteenth, May thirteenth, and June first. Deliverables look like this. It is a five-page report. These elements are included in it. Good examples of report look like... Poor examples look like... I will be checking in with you midpoint on each of these to see how the work is progressing. What I expect to see at those particular times is an outline that shows which areas you are going to be covering in the report and the progress so far."

Josette would respond, "Do you want me to check in on a weekly basis to give you a quick update?"

Rita would say, "Absolutely. I want to know if things are going according to plan, how your resources are holding up, and what challenges you need to address. So, let's review. What have you heard me say?"

This type of detail gave Josette an extremely clear idea of what was expected of her, and gave each of Rita's direct reports a chance to respond.

ONGOING ENGAGEMENT

When a spacecraft is sent to the moon, thousands of course corrections are made along the way to make sure it reaches its target. When you have a Real Conversation about "How am I doing? How can I improve?" think of your feedback as the way to make course corrections to make sure you reach your shared goals. It is obvious that once-a-year events dedicated to feedback can't keep the course on track from month to month. Ongoing support and clarification needs to happen regularly. It will not only help you keep things running smoothly, but will avert most of the situations where drastic measures are necessary.

Once clear outcomes are established, provide people with input along the way to help keep them on track. Engaging in this Real Conversation frequently and with positive intention is one of the most productive ways you can build a successful organization. Why? Giving individuals ongoing feedback informs and inspires them with a sense of continuity and shared purpose. It also raises their morale and productivity, and plainly feels good! You simply cannot expect people to change without input. It is amazing how a few well-chosen words, not just the good or the bad stuff, spoken in the right context, can lift someone up to not only recognize their strengths but also encourage them to make the changes that will enhance their ability to achieve results.

Often you may want to give constructive input to someone, but fear negative consequences. Or you may fear that if you give criticism to someone, you are inviting yourself to be criticized. The bottom line is this: if you do not give feedback, there is a good chance things will not improve or may even get worse. In addition, you will lose credibility with the high performers who might think you lack the guts to have the Real Conversation with the low performers. These negative perceptions form the basis for disengagement and, ultimately, lower performance.

Questions like "Why didn't you tell me when it happened?" or "Why didn't you just let me know I was going down the wrong road?" will come up less and less when you nip the issues as they arise. Delayed feedback results in a backlog of muddled and dark feelings, and the longer you wait, the larger the negative emotional wake.

The high performers in your organization need feedback as well. Often a high performer will benefit from being asked, "Where do you think you can improve?" Once you hear the answer, then you can ask, "Would you like some coaching on that point?" By asking these two questions, you can provide the right feedback for that person.

Some people use the dump-truck approach to feedback. They simply dump it out like a pile of dirt and think they have done the job. Remember, to make feedback a Real Conversation, you need to be present with the person, tell them the truth, and be engaged in a two-way conversation based in positive intent.

When you envision the person you are speaking with in a positive light, you set the tone for more trust and respect. Take a moment and visualize in your mind's eye someone with whom you need to speak. See him as a success. Consider his strengths and goodwill. Remember, you are giving feedback so that person can do his job. You are committed to making sure he receives the feedback in the spirit that is positive. This technique is a good way to prepare for all of your Real Conversations, but this one in particular.

Typically, the word "feedback" holds a negative charge. People think, "Oh no, I'm going to be put down, criticized, shredded." Taking the time to re-spin the feedback changes the meaning into something helpful. Think of feedback as equaling "input," or "course correction," and you will find your Real Conversations go a lot smoother.

Here is an example of feedback first given from negative and then positive intent. Put yourself in Bill's shoes and imagine what your reaction might be.

"Bill, I have heard some feedback that you are up to your old tricks again, and it is just not working. How many times do we have to go over this for you to get it? Are you trying to give our unit a bad name? You just can't barge into people's offices and make demands of them, especially with the senior executives. They say you are rude and offensive."

TAKE TWO

"Bill, I have just heard some feedback that concerns me. Several months ago, we discussed the communication pattern that you employ. You know, you just drop into the senior executives' offices and make demands of them. After our conversation, you stopped, set up meetings, and made a great improvement. Sadly, I am beginning to get feedback that you have been showing up again, unannounced. What is going on for you?"

Frank had quarterly semi-informal discussions with his direct reports. He began, "I want to get a general sense of how all of you think you are doing, say, over the past couple of months. Are you meeting, exceeding, or below your own expectations?"

Frank encouraged his people to take a few minutes to talk about their self-perceptions. After listening to them fully, he couched his input in their terms, conversationally saying, "One thing I have observed in that area is..." and "A suggestion I have in that area is..." The entire Real Conversation often took place over lunch, and it was a casual way that he could both provide and receive quality information. Then he would say, "How can I better support you? How can I be a better manager of your process? What is it that you need from me? If I could change one thing to be a better boss for you, what should that be?"

Frank's direct reports always felt motivated after these lively meetings. By the time their annual performance reviews took place, a solid foundation had been established that encouraged open, direct communication. Rarely did anyone run into issues that blindsided them. Quarterly is usually a good interval to have this Real Conversation, unless, of course, the situation arises when people begin to veer off-course.

"Your expectations open or close the doors of your supply.
If you expect grand things, and work honestly for them,
they will come to you, your supply will correspond
with your expectation."
—Orison Swett Marden

"Feedback is the breakfast of champions."
— Ken Blanchard

FEEDBACK STYLES

The intention for providing input/feedback is to enhance performance. Everyone has a preferred way of receiving feedback, and people can differ dramatically in what they are able or willing to hear and process. Think of all the different styles of feedback as a menu of lunch sandwiches. It is invaluable for you to know your own preferences as well as which of your reports likes a BLT over a club! (Note: Most employees spend months or more walking on eggshells trying to figure out their bosses' feedback style. Save your staff a lot of time by telling them early on what works for you.) As you read the menu below, keep in mind that you can mix and match.

One of the best ways to shrink your blind spots is to pro-actively see feedback from other people. It doesn't matter whether it is at work or in your personal life; the goal in receiving feedback is to create congruity. You want the perception of how you see yourself to match with how others see you. Now, whether you are receiving feedback or giving feedback, it is really important to understand the different feedback styles. Everyone likes to receive feedback in slightly different ways. When you can determine what your preferred feedback style is and identify the preferred feedback style of others, you can let others know what your style is, and also, when there is an opportunity for you to give feedback to others, that you can respond in kind.

Imagine that the different feedback styles are like different types of sandwiches:

PLAIN SANDWICH

This is the classic feedback style. "Give me a hug, tell me what I did wrong, give me another hug." In other words, the feedback is preceded by positive strokes. Let the person know how much they are valued, how much you like them, how much you care about them. Then give them the message or items that they can correct or improve on and then finish the feedback by giving them some more positive strokes. This is kind of like the classic sandwich method of giving people feedback, and it works with some people, but not for everyone.

OPEN FACE SANDWICH

In the open-face, the first step is you acknowledge the work that they did. Let them know what you thought they were to trying to accomplish so that they can understand that you are on the same page. Let them know specifically what they did and the impact that it had in those areas that need improvement. Then follow that up with some suggestions on how you think that they could do it better. The Open-Faced Sandwich feedback style sets up a different type of rapport at the beginning. You let them know that you are thinking along the same lines about the intention/outcome of what they did. This step helps validate the feedback and also provides them with some concrete suggestions on how to improve.

FINGER SANDWICH

This approach involves just giving the person one piece of feedback at a time. This style works for the person who is really busy and has a lot on their plate; excuse the pun. The Finger Sandwich lets them have just one thing to focus on, the one thing that will make the biggest difference. It can be very refreshing to have just one thing rather than inundating them with a long list of suggestions.

CLUB SANDWICH

This approach is very direct. It is not fluffing them up, it is not trying to make them feel good, it is simply telling them in a respectful way what they did, what the problem as and that is all, no more. You don't have to finish the feedback with a hug or suggestions. People who like the Club Sandwich just want to hear what it is.

SUBMARINE SANDWICH

It is time to prepare for the deep dive. You will need to sit down with this person for an hour and work through all the details of what they did and what they could do better. Really be prepared with good notes so that when they walk away they take something solid that is locked down and clear.

FEEDBACK BEST PRACTICES

1. **Feedback is best when served fresh.**
    Give feedback as soon as possible so you are not
    waiting days, months, years to talk. Otherwise,
    ideas and suggestions will just circle round and
    round in your head and drain your energy. When
    it is fresh in your head it can be fresh in their
    minds, and you can come up with a real workable
    resolution and save yourself a lot of pain.

2. **Let them know the meal is coming.**
    Ask the individual when a good time is to talk. Re-
    quest their full attention. Make your appointment
    close in time to when you made your request for

a meeting. You might say, "When would be a good time for us to sit down and talk for a few minutes about how we work together?" Or you might say, "I wanted to give you some feedback about your presentation." Or, "Something happened the other day and we just need to sit down and work it through." Again, it is best to do this meeting as soon as possible after you make that request.

3. **Feedback is best when delivered in person.** Give it to the person directly or talk to them on the phone. Feedback is a two-way communication, not a drive-by or dump truck. Definitely do not try to resolve a conflict by email. *Email is the worst way to resolve conflicts* because you have no voice tone, facial expressions, or two-way exchange.

PREPARE TO GIVE AND RECEIVE FEEDBACK

If someone is off target and misses the mark, feedback is usually required to get folks back on track. It is important to take issues directly to the person rather than gossip and create negative conspiracies. Think about it, wouldn't you rather hear the issue directly from the person over hearing second or third hand?

If you are really upset sometimes it can be useful to have someone coach you prior to your taking an issue to a person. This is different from creating gossip and negative conspiracies. Your coach can run you through the "Getting to Positive Intention" (page) process and then provide a follow-up check after you have had the conversation. This will help you reset the emotional button because when you are giving feedback, you want to give it from a place of neutrality and opportunity to reconnect with that person.

Giving feedback requires that you come, to make the point again, from neutrality. Then you need to take the situation/issue apart and determine your perception of it. Then it is important to ask the other person for their perception of the conflict and together you can plan what is the best way forward.

ACKNOWLEDGE AND BACKTRACK

Martin gave Bill some difficult feedback about Bill's lack of performance. After hearing his boss lay out some feedback, Bill responded, "Well, it really sounds like you are just condemning everything I do." Martin said, "Let's go back a couple of steps. What did I say that led you to that conclusion?"

Bill answered, "Well, you blasted me on all fronts."

Martin said, "I addressed three distinct issues. The other areas are all fine. I'm not saying everything is wrong. It's just necessary that I point out what isn't working and offer specific suggestions that I believe will help."

If somebody you speak with has a strong visceral reaction to the conversation, stop, backtrack, and ask her what she is experiencing right then and there. It will help keep things from boiling over. It can happen that she is not hearing the message that you are intending, and by backtracking, you can see where her interpretation of what you said went sideways. Then you can clarify. Being present and actively responding to the person you are talking to creates a safe place for others to express what is actually going on for them. At the end of your Real Conversation, ask, "With what are you walking away?" This way you can verify that your intended message has been received.

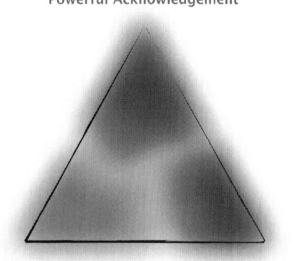

Powerful Acknowledgement

Go to the Source   Clean-up

FEEDBACK TRILOGY

GO TO THE SOURCE

The formula for giving feedback to an individual is:

1. State your intention. Let the person know you want to talk to them to enhance or improve the relationship.

2. From an Observer's point of view, let them know specifically what happened. Relay the facts of what they either said or did.

3. Separate what you hear from your interpretation of what happened. Then share how you interpret

what went on and how it impacted you. Share what thoughts you were left with.

4. Ask them what was going on for them so that you've got an opportunity to understand where they were coming from. This is the opportunity for you to connect with their positive intent.

5. Together decide what you want to do. You want to strategize a way to move forward if this type of situation ever comes up again. What will make the relationship better rather than repeat a situation filled with stress and tension?

CLEAN-UP

Clean-up is another type of feedback or communication you might have with somebody when you inadvertently create damage in an exchange.

To clean up:

1. Be accountable for what happened.

2. Apologize. Do not give an excuse. Some people think a good excuse adds to the apology — it does not.

3. Make a commitment that next time you will do it differently if a similar situation occurs.

4. Let the other know that your relationship is important.

Make sure you make a genuine apology. Do not just pay lip service to the process. When you apologize, the intention is to reset the relationship. Some people will immediately accept your apology and are ready to move on. Others may wait to see if you "walk the talk" before they restore trust in you. Regardless, you need to be able to be able to "walk the talk" and be prepared to be tested by those people who need behavioral evidence to believe you mean what you say.

POWERFUL ACKNOWLEDGMENT

Powerful Acknowledgment is a way to provide positive reinforcement. It is catching the person doing something right. It feels really, really good when you can tell somebody about what they did really well.

Three steps for giving acknowledgment are:

1. Let the person know specifically what they did. Don't generalize by saying, "Nice job," but let them know specifically what they did.

2.   Let them know the impact that it had on your personally, how it made you feel, how it touched you, how it made a difference for you.

3.   Let them know what you are looking forward to in the future. This really sets a positive pathway. When you acknowledge somebody, it is great to do it in person, even in private. Then again, others like this kind of appreciation in public. Acknowledging people also works well over email. You can also use the opportunity to cc other people and let them know what a good job they did.

RECEIVE FEEDBACK
WITH AN OPEN MIND

When you receive feedback, remember it is not always perfect. The person may blurt something out or may say something that pushes your buttons and upsets you. Feedback requires a place of mutual understanding. Receiving feedback is a good time to assume positive intention because when somebody comes to you with feedback, they want the relationship to get better. There is positive intention on both sides of the feedback equation, in the giving and the receiving of it.

WALK AND TALK

When you take issues to a person for feedback, do clean up, and acknowledge on a regular basis you will keep your bubble of experience permeable and expanding. Your relationships will also be much healthier.

You can take these three communication skills and put them to practice at work in the form of what is called a walk-and-talk. A walk-and-talk is a conversation that you have with somebody and the intention is to enhance your relationship.

The Real Conversation Walk-n-Talk

"My intention is to enhance our working relationship."

Our Feedback Styles — What works, doesn't work

Clean-up

"I apologize for...."

Take it to the Source

"An issue that diminishes our effectiveness is...."

Coaching

"What should I start or stop doing to be more effective in working with you?"

"How can I support you?"

Acknowledgment

"One thing I appreciate about working with you..."

We recommend actually going on a physical walk with the person. When you are walking with somebody you can leave the old issues behind; you can work through things; you keep a sense of movement; you are creating the future together. Walk-and-talks are on your little menu card here and it is really easy. This is one of those practices that you can just incorporate into your weekly communications with people.

It is a nice metaphor for a way to work through the issues. The way the walk-and-talk works is that you just follow the menu on the back of your meal card. You can refer to it; it works like a back-and-forth, or a ping-pong. "Let's go on a walk-and-talk for fifteen minutes; grab your card and let's work the menu going back and forth."

So that the walk-and-talk is successful it is important that each of you knows each other's feedback style. Then you can ask, "OK, is there anything I need to clean up?" If there is Clean-up then both clean up what you need to and commit to move forward into straight talk.

Take it to the Source includes things such as, "Are there any issues that affect how we work together?" An example could be that you are on a project and the rules are not really clear and you are stepping on each other's toes. You could say, "Let us have a talk about what you are going to do, what I am going to do, and you just kind of work it through. Do you have any coaching for me?" because it is easy to give somebody coaching by asking for it.

It's appropriate to employ the "Finger Sandwich" approach here. That means you can say, "OK, how could I be more effective? Or, "If I could start or stop doing something that would make me more effective in working with you, what would that be?" That gives you something really just to focus on. What keeps you up at night? What are your concerns? Maybe you have a tight timeline and you are just wondering if you are going to be able to get all the work done within that timeline.

Let the person know what your goals are; how you are trying to develop just as an individual. Or somebody inside a business or operation might say, "You know, one of the things that I am working on is listening better. So, if we are in a conversation and it seems like I am kind of wanting to veer off to something else, just give me one of these and I'll slow down and try to tune in."

How can I support you? This is a great question to ask somebody. How can I support you to be more effective in your job? What can I do to help you out? Talk about collaboration. This is one of the fundamental questions that will open up that discussion. And then lastly, acknowledgment; one thing that you appreciate about working with that person. Again, we want to end the walk-and-talk on a positive note and this is a really good way to just let that person know what you appreciate about working with them.

CONSIDER THIS:

1. How do you express your expectations to your team? How would you know if you have been clear and complete?

2. What is the feedback style of the people with whom you work? Do you vary how you give feedback, and how much?

3. What are the Real Conversations about feedback that you avoid? What is it you need to make Real Conversations happen?

"Negative feedback is better than none.
I would rather have a man hate me than overlook me.
As long as he hates me I make a difference."
— Hugh Prather

"You don't have to be better than everyone else. You just have to be better than you thought you ever could be."
—Ken Venturi

COACHING
FOR PROFESSIONAL
DEVELOPMENT

People in your organization sign up for far more than a nine-to-five "do work and go home" robotic job description. They want to develop themselves personally and professionally. They want to advance in compensation and responsibility. When you initiate the Real Conversation, "How will I be developed?" it demonstrates that you are truly committed to the growth and progress of everyone, and it enhances morale and job retention as well.

Most people wait for their leader to step up and engage them in this discussion about their growth and progress. If as a manager or director you feel uncomfortable about having a conversation about development possibilities with your people, remember that having to replace people who are good performers costs far more than the momentary worries about sitting down for a face-to-face. All Real Conversations require being present, telling the truth, expressing positive intent, and creating a two-way street. By now, you probably have some practice, comfort, and even expertise in employing these key elements. "How will I be developed?" is the one Real Conversation in business that requires more negotiation, dialogue, or two-way street interaction than the rest. This is an opportunity to actively engage your people rather than showing up with all of the answers.

"How will I be developed?" is a question that is asked and answered as soon as you bring someone on board. It addresses a number of issues including compensation, promotion, and training options. Many leaders wait all year for the big annual performance review to talk about development and promotion issues. It is best to have one-on-ones prior to that event, and then inside the performance review, to address development before you discuss objectives. People want to know where they stand and how to get ahead first.

Jenny expresses her interest and commitment to her staff by saying, "I believe that your development is going to be the key to our success. Let's talk about how you would like to be developed next year and then we will cover your personal objectives." Jenny likes to have development conversations at least twice a year, as well as after large projects, in terms of developmental debriefings. Linking development to projects is a valuable way to maximize the learning aspects of project work. This is a very useful practice when you have limited dollars for development.

FOCUS ON STRENGTHS

"What is the plan for development?" will allow you to focus on a person's strengths rather than harping on their weaknesses. Not everyone is good at everything. Rather than trying to fill a weak gap with development, you should identify strong areas of work and encourage him or her to become even more robust. A strengths-based discussion has a very powerful base and usually is much more motivating. Which sounds better to you? "We have identified three areas where you are weak (challenged/ need development) and want you to take some classes to bring you up to speed." Or "We have identified three areas that you are particularly strong in and want to build on your strengths by having you take some classes."

Oliver, a section director, engaged Victor in a Real Conversation based on Victor's strengths.

Oliver: "I want to get a sense of what you see as your strengths and then how you see yourself taking your strengths to the next level."

Victor: "Well, three things come to mind in terms of my strengths, strategic thinking, open communication, and managing cross-functional teams and projects. I have seen this course on strategic planning and implementation that has gotten good reviews. I would like to take that course next year. Then afterwards, I could hold a lunch and learn where I could present the course highlights."

Oliver: "Sounds very promising. Could you consider sharing/teaching what you learn as a way of integrating the learning?"

Victor: "Sure. I would like to start a best practices forum for cross-functional managers across the business unit. That would be a great way for me to learn even more and to share what I know. It would also help us network across the larger functional areas. I can't think of anything to enhance open communication. I think that is just how I operate. Do you have any ideas?"

Oliver: "There is a good book called *Daring to Have Real Conversations in Business.* You might want to read it and then go to the book club and talk about how it could be used in our division."

Victor: "Yeah, I've heard it's a really good book."

Oliver: "OK, I think you have come up with some fine ideas. Will that satisfy you for next year, or is there any other area you want to develop?"

Victor: "I'm good. I will write this up in my performance plan and have it to you by the end of the week."

TRANSPARENCY

It is important to be transparent, meaning totally upfront, when you discuss development issues. Let people know the constraints and challenges with which you are dealing, whether they are monetary, time, or something else. Try not to protect them from the truth. Doing so will most likely be perceived as withholding, even with the best of intentions. Naturally, certain circumstances require a more sensitive treatment of data. In those times you can say, "There is other information that I am not at liberty to share with you at this moment. I will communicate it with all of you at the earliest practical time."

Margaret, a director of business development, told her management team, "As you know, our sales figures have been down for the last two quarters. One of the consequences of having to tighten our belts is that we have had to make severe cuts in our expenditures. Unfortunately, one area that has been virtually eliminated is training and development. I was disappointed to hear that news because I know some of you were expecting to take some courses promised to you last year. I share your disappointment. To be honest, I was looking forward to gaining new information from your training, but this is how it has turned out. I am committed to creating opportunities for your growth and development regardless of the budget, and I plan to talk about development plans with each of you individually. Please join in and come up with some innovative solutions to this hopefully temporary situation. Next week at three o'clock, I would like to meet with anyone who wants to brainstorm."

Margaret accomplished two important pieces of business. By being transparent and sharing the truth of the situation, she opened up the creative opportunity for her team to rise up and engage together. People quickly formulated an efficient way to rotate within their jobs, which allowed them to broaden their expertise, did not cost anything, and satisfied them individually because they were part of the solution.

PROMOTIONS ARE NOT CHECK THE BOX

There will be times when an employee will ask you directly, "What do I have to do to get a promotion?" This person thinks that getting promoted is akin to a to-do list. All they have to do is check the box and they set up in a new office! You can get trapped if you are not careful with your answer.

Sheldon is a mid-level manager. Jeff approached him casually in the hallway. "Hey, Shel, what do I have to do to get a promotion?" Sheldon suggested they set up a meeting on development the next morning.

> Sheldon: "I am getting the sense that you perceive a promotion as a cut-and-dry process, kind of like you do x, y, and z, and voilà, you advance. Am I close?"

> Jeff: "Actually, getting promoted seems to me like a moving target. Each year I am told something different about how to do it, so I just want to nail it down."

> Sheldon: "I can understand your desire to know what is needed to move to the next level. Each year is different, you are right, because our business is different every year. If we relied on what made us successful last year, we would be in serious trouble as things change. That is how it is with promotions. It is a fluid process, and just be-

cause someone got promoted last year does not mean that another person with the same accomplishments would get a promotion the following year."

Jeff: "That sounds a bit confusing."

Sheldon: "Well, in order to keep our edge, we must continually raise the bar. And if you are just focused on the bar, you will always be frustrated because those people who do get promoted are the ones who aim higher than the bar; they exceed expectations."

Jeff: "Thanks for explaining how you approach development."

Often an employee feels that he is due a promotion when you do not agree. It is critical that you set realistic expectations in your Real Conversation. Sometimes the problem is simply a timeframe difference. He may be expecting a promotion in one year, and you see it's going to take four years. It is important to be able to clearly say, "I see this progression taking longer than you do and this is where and how it's going to take longer." Then spell it out for him and give him opportunities to react and ask questions. Listen, respond, and clarify. Take it in increments. Keep the conversation cycle open so that you are constantly tracking how he is listening to and understanding what it is that you are saying.

Sandra gave new people coming on board her team a clear and effective presentation about how promotions happen.

"I want to take a few minutes to go over the process that we follow for performance. As a rule, only 10 percent of the people who have been at their current grade level for three years are eligible for a grade-level promotion. We have four grade levels, A, B, C, and D. Also, five bands are within each grade, numbered one to five. The B grade consists of vice presidents and directors, the C grade is for managers, and the D grade is the line. It is possible to advance within your grade level every year. Grade-level promotions are more difficult to attain. For a grade-level promotion, the candidate who had met the performance criteria of exceeding expectations in all the categories in their grade for two out of three years will be placed in a pool. Then those candidates are ranked.

"Approximately 30 percent of those candidates receive promotions. You can receive a band-level promotion annually based on your performance. In order to receive a band-level increase, your peers must consider your performance exceptional. I want to emphasize that you get a promotion based on exceptional performance. Do not expect a promotion based on time spent working at your job. It just does not happen that way. You need to be proactive in adding value to the company. Now, before we go on I'd like to have you feed back to me what you have heard so far."

Presenting this type of clear explanation, often with a chart on the front end, makes everything much easier later on in the game.

DEAL WITH DISAPPOINTMENT

You can expect that you will encounter disappointments as well as celebrations when you address development. It is important to be able to handle potentially emotional situations in a businesslike fashion. When an individual faces the fact that their plans are not going to happen the way they imagined, disappointment is a natural reaction. Hang in there with them and say, "I can understand how this may seem like a setback for you. However, what encourages me is that I see that you are taking this seriously. There are ways you can turn this around." Put a positive frame around disappointment. Remember, high expectations demonstrate commitment and desire to add value.

DISAPPOINTMENT-BASED UNREAL CONVERSATION

Here is another example of handling disappointment, this time around promotion letdowns.

Jane is a successful leader who has reported to Ted for the last year and a half. She has worked in a couple of business units in another division for six years and in an eight-year career has progressed to manager level. Although Jane is successful, competent, and generally well-regarded, it is unlikely that she will achieve promotion to the director level. There are other people at her level who are simply more qualified. Jane expects that she will be promoted and is unaware that her assumed career progression will be thwarted.

> Ted: "We haven't really talked about your long-term goals for your career, and I'd like to get a sense of your expectations for the next five years. You have been working here for the last six years at the manager level, and I want to make sure we are on the same page in terms of your development."
>
> Jane: "Thank you for asking. My prior bosses never asked me that question in such a direct way. I have been thinking about what is next for me for quite a while. The step to a director level is a big one, and for the last four years, I have been happy where I am because I have younger kids at home and did not want to do the travel required for that

position. But now I think I am ready to consider that step. I think my performance ratings have been pretty good and I'm ready to move up."

Ted: "I'm glad we are having this talk. I did not know you were intentionally keeping your position stable over the last four years. As you know, Stan is moving over to Procurement, and his director's position will come open in six months."

Jane: "Yes, I know. I was thinking that might be a good opportunity for me to step up."

Ted: "To be honest, the timing for Stan's position is not quite right for you. There have been a couple of other people who have been preparing for that position over the past two years."

Jane: "How come they have been preparing and I have not?"

Ted: "It is really up to you to proactively seek out that track. And it makes sense that, because you have been keeping your position stable, you would not be seeking a change of that magnitude. Now that you are, we can begin the process of preparation."

Jane: "So, this could take a while."

Ted: "Yes, it could. Many people don't realize what it takes to make the jump from manager to director, and once they have that goal, we can lay out a plan so that the expectations are clear and level-set."

Jane: "How long do you think it will take me to be ready?"

Ted: "That is a difficult question. Much of that depends on you and how you want to work. It could take you anywhere between two and five years."

Jane: "Oh."

Ted: "I sense that you were expecting a different timeline."

Jane: "Well, six months to five years is a huge gap. It is just hard to think it will take that long, and there is no guarantee that I will get promoted even after two-plus years."

Ted: "What can I do to support you? I want you to be motivated at work and I want to be realistic as well. Sometimes those two goals are tricky to balance."

Jane: "Well, I definitely feel we are being realistic. I'm not ready quite yet."

Ted: "I think that once we have laid out the specifics, you will see why I put that range on the timeline. You will also be able to move forward and that will help."

"We cannot teach people anything; we can only help them discover it within themselves."
— Galileo Galilei

COACHING FOR PERFORMANCE IMPROVEMENT

Here are several scenarios of having the Real Conversation, "How am I doing? How can I improve?" They are Real Conversations of people in organizations just like yours. Imagine how you can take the examples and personalize them to fit specific performance situations you are dealing with right now.

Meet:

1. The High Performer

2. The Medium Steady State Performer

3. The Low Performer

4. Peer to Peer Exchanges

5. Special Situations

REAL CONVERSATION WITH A HIGH PERFORMER

Tom scheduled a meeting with one of his high performers, Bill, for a performance review.

Tom: "Bill, fortunately for you this will be a very short meeting. You are doing a great job. Your clients are happy and you are on budget. I am delighted with your performance."

Bill: "Great, thank you. Is there anything else?"

Tom: "What do you mean?"

Bill: "Well, how can I improve?"

Tom: "That is a good question, but I can't think of anything. You are the ideal employee. I wish I had more like you. Enjoy your day; you deserve it."

While Tom's intention was to compliment Bill, you can see that something was missing for him. It is nice to be complimented, but Bill wanted something more in-depth.

Often, high performers just get positive feedback. That can lead to thinking, "That is all well and good, but there must be a place where I can grow." There can also be a sense of "What are you not telling me?" or "You don't really care about my development." It is true that you want to acknowledge their high performance to motivate them, but you also need to create a learning edge, a challenge, along with the positive support.

Debra, a sales manager, started her meeting with Sally, one of her direct reports, by saying, "Sally, I am happy that we have this opportunity to review your performance this quarter. Without a doubt, you are outstanding. To what do you attribute your success?" By starting on a positive note, and then asking the person to self-reflect, you are setting the foundation for a two-way dialogue. After Sally finished, Debra went on to say, "These are the three key strengths that I see that you have... The area that you have shown the most growth in is this area.... How do you think you could leverage your other strengths?" She again elicited Sally's response.

Debra's entire focus is on Sally's strengths, not her weaknesses. "What activities can we do in the next quarter to develop your other strengths?" Debra's intention is to enroll Sally in creating the plan.

Sally: "I'd like to be involved in some of the more complicated sales negotiations. Can I attend some of those meetings with you?"

Debra: "I had not thought of that, and it seems like a good idea. You would have to attend the briefing sessions prior to the meetings, and you could do that by teleconference if you are in the field."

Sally: "That sounds great. I think I would learn a lot."

Debra: "In addition to those meetings, since you are so strong in these areas, I want you to think about how you can mentor at least one other person in the sales organization. I have a couple of people in mind, specifically Tom and Frieda. How would you feel about working with either of them?"

Sally: "What would that look like?"

Debra: "It will take you one hour every three weeks to do case review with them."

Sally: "It is a bit of a stretch time-wise, but I will make it work. I think I would work better with Tom."

Debra: "OK, then I will let him know to contact you." When do you think it would a good time to check in on how you are doing with mentoring Tom?"

Sally: "How about after three times of meeting with him?"

Debra: "OK. Thanks for this meeting. I think we have come up with some viable options for your next steps."

REAL CONVERSATION WITH A HIGH PERFORMER WITH ISSUES

Tony has a good performance record as manager of a team and has a strong reputation for delivery and getting results. However, his team finds him to be reactive when he is under pressure. He becomes didactic, a little arrogant, and impatient. Tony's style creates an uneasy, unpredictable atmosphere, and as a consequence, people avoid talking to him about it.

Charlene, Tony's manager, knows that she needs to tackle this persistent alienating behavior.

> Charlene: "Tony, I am glad that we have an hour to talk. I'd like to get some input from you in terms of how you think you are doing and reflect to you some of my observations. Then we can brainstorm some of the possible ways to move forward. First of all, you have a strong performance record and I know I can count on you to deliver on the results that you promise. This gives me a great

deal of confidence. How would you say you account for your repeated successes?"

Tony: "I think is it a matter of focus. I stay focused on the goal until it is done."

Charlene: "That is great. How is your team doing? I mean, you are meeting the goals, but how are they doing as a team?"

Tony: "It seems that there is a little stress, but we deal with it."

Charlene: "Tell me a little more about how you deal with it.

Tony: "I give them time to vent, and then we move on."

Charlene: "OK, the stress part matches what I have been observing and hearing from people in your team."

Tony: "What do you mean?"

Charlene: "I see that when you get focused on a goal, you lose some of your perspective on what is going on around you. In my team meetings, you sometimes get impatient, and it seems like you stop listening."

Tony: "Yeah, you are right."

Charlene: "A couple of your direct reports have come to me saying that they have a hard time approaching you."

Tony: "But I tell them my door is open."

Charlene: "Yes, your door is open, but are you really there to listen and respond? They are intimidated by your impatience. You can cut them off mid-sentence."

Tony: "Wow, I never mean to."

Charlene: "Yes, this is definitely a blind spot for you. What do you think you can do to shrink it?"

Tony: "Hmm, I'm not sure yet."

Charlene: "One thing that comes to mind for me is that when you and I do your goal setting, I want to double check with you that I am not overloading you. I have grown accustomed to giving you more and more, but it crosses my mind that you may be overburdened. Maybe that pressure gets translated to your team."

Tony: "It makes sense. I have just taken whatever you gave me and charged on."

Charlene: "Yes, a strength that you have, but now the cost is becoming too high."

Tony: "I think I will let my team know we have had this talk. Perhaps we can come up with a way I can be alerted when I am pressing too much. I also need to be more aware of my team when I am feeling pressured. That is easier said than done."

Charlene: "Is there anything else that comes to mind in terms of what you can do?"

Tony: "Not really, but I think we should check in two weeks from now and I can let you know how my talk with the team went, and perhaps they will have some good ideas."

Charlene: "OK, sounds good. I am glad we had a chance to go over this. You seem open to the topic and willing to take a look at yourself. That's great. Let's meet in two weeks. "

Tony: "Absolutely."

Charlene took the time to give Tony specific examples to help him metabolize the feedback. Had she said, "Tony you are pressuring your people, and it has to stop," he might have recoiled into a defensive position and it would have taken a lot longer for him to be open to making changes.

REAL CONVERSATION WITH A MEDIUM/STEADY STATE PERFORMER

Fred, a commercial strategy director, is doing the basics, but not much more. He has been in the role for five years and wants to move to the next grade level in pay. He has been getting decent performance ratings by his previous bosses, delivering on most objectives, but no one sees him as a key contributor or as going further.

Fred: "I was really looking forward to our quarterly review."

Jim: "I am glad to hear that because sometimes I think there might be a gap in how each of us sees your performance. Why don't you start, and tell me what you were looking forward to talking about."

Fred: "OK. As you know I have been in this position for the last five years. My two previous bosses gave me good performance ratings, and I feel it is close to the time for getting the next grade level."

Jim: "What is the basis upon which you think you should be promoted?"

Fred: "I have been at this level for five years, and I think my performance has been consistent."

Jim: "Are you aware of the process that we use to evaluate who gets a promotion?"

Fred: "I think all the names go into a pool based on current grade level and performance ratings."

Jim: "Something like that. Actually, each manager has to present their people for promotion, and a percentage of those who are most qualified get the promotion."

Fred: "OK."

Jim: "You know, Fred, you have reasonable scores, but what is missing is what would set you apart from other people at your level. You do your work. There is no doubt about that. In order to get a promotion, though, you actually have to be working at the next level for about six months. Your performance has been at a steady state for the past two years. You have not taken on any extra assignments and you have not done exceptional work on any projects so far. Your work history is consistent, as you have stated, but in order to get promoted, it needs to increase."

Fred: "No one ever told me that my work was substandard."

Jim: "OK, let's back up a second. I did not say your work was substandard. It is not at the level needed for a promotion."

Fred: "Oh. So it is not enough just to do your job around here."

Jim: "It seems that something has shifted for you. I heard it in the tone of your last statement. What are you hearing me say and what is your reaction to it?"

Fred: "Well, it seems like I have worked hard over the last five years, and now, when it is time for promotion, I am being told that hard work is not enough. That is pretty de-motivating."

Jim: "Let's take some time to talk through this. I can understand that this can feel de-motivating. I realize that you have not had this type of feedback by your prior managers."

Fred: "That is for sure."

Jim: "For that omission, I apologize. I realize that prior to my arrival you thought, in your mind, you were performing at a level worthy of promotion."

Fred: "Yes."

Jim: "Now you understand more of where you are and I want to review with you what will be needed in terms of your performance to reach the next level."

Fred: "You mean that I could still get promoted?"

Jim: "That is up to you. Unfortunately, people don't get promoted just for working hard. Working hard is what is expected. What gets you promoted is exceptional performance."

Fred: "What does that mean?"

Jim: "If everyone is working hard, then we need to have a way to separate out who is adding more value. This could be in terms of special projects, discovering a new way that we can work that makes us more productive, innovations that put us on the leading edge, that kind of thing."

Fred: "OK. So, I need to create something that separates me from the rest of my peers."

Jim: "Yes. You remember Francine. She created a new way to process tickets that make us 30 percent more efficient, and on top of that, her unit had the highest productivity scores for two years."

Fred: "So, this could take me two more years?"

Jim: "It could. We are looking for high performance that is sustained and additional value that you add."

Fred: "I don't have any ideas right now of how I can do that."

Jim: "I will help you come up with some projects and activities that will get you on your way. You don't have to do this alone. It is my job to help you succeed and get a promotion."

Fred: "Phew."

Jim: "So, can you recap what you have heard and where you are with what I have said?"

Fred: "Basically, my work has met expectations over the past few years, but that is not enough to get a promotion. I need to have a sustained increase of value that I add to the company in order to be promoted."

Jim: "Right. And what are your thoughts about all that?"

Fred: "Well, I was frustrated at first, but now I have a better sense that you are supporting me to get the promotion. I am still a little discouraged by the fact it may take me two years. That seems like a long time."

Jim: "OK. It seems like we are on the same page now, and although you are a little discouraged, I feel that there is a possibility for your advancement, and that was not the case before this conversation. I think we should meet in a week and talk about projects that you might get involved with to start your progress. How does that sound to you?"

Fred: "Sounds fine. Thanks for talking with me."

REAL CONVERSATION
WITH A LOW PERFORMER

Frieda used this approach with Kelly, who had a very direct communication style and whose performance was in jeopardy.

> Frieda: "I am glad that we have this chance to talk and meet to discuss how work is going for you. I remember from our last meeting that you like your feedback direct."
>
> Kelly: "Yes, that's right."
>
> Frieda: "I have a few concerns that I would like to get on the table and see what we can come up with between us. There are two specific issues regarding how you work and/or the results that you are producing that need to change. One, your reports are always three to four days late, and they are sloppily written. And two, customers are complaining about your phone skills. Let's take a few minutes to scope in on each of these, and I would like to understand what your perceptions are, define a few focus areas, and together we can create a plan to address these areas."

Frieda did not beat around the bush. She put the news on the table and opened up the discussion. Although this direct style may be overpowering for some, people with a direct communication style will appreciate the fact that you get right to the point. In most situations, it works best to ask the person for their perceptions first to help minimize the possibility for a defensive reaction. You can see that once you hear what the other person has to say, it gives you a chance to see where the openings are and how you can link your perceptions to their comments.

DISRUPTIVE BEHAVIOR CONVERSATION

Stephen, a director of operations, had set up a meeting to discuss Paul's recent behavior at work. Paul has been in his current role for six years and in the last four months has become disruptive, often obstructive, and negative about individual team members and other departments. People have told Stephen that Paul is not "pulling his weight" and "tends to keep to himself."

Stephen's style was direct, and he was always comfortable putting the issues right out there.

> Stephen: "I know that I have not been your manager for very long, but during the four months I have been, I have noticed a marked change in your behavior and your impact on others. Specifically, it seems like you are engaging in hallway conversations that seem to have a negative impact on others. Usually, you are a very positive person. I am wondering if you were aware of this, and I am curious about what is happening for you at work."

Paul: "This catches me by surprise because I did not realize I was having that negative of an impact."

Stephen: "Yes, three people have come to me after talking with you in the break room saying that you are really talking negatively about the Marketing department and a few people in our department."

Paul: "This is very embarrassing because I recall making a few remarks, but I did not realize that it was having that kind of impact."

Stephen: "Well, yes, it has. You know that the relationship has been strained with Marketing and we have been doing a lot of work to patch things up with them, so when you are blasting them in public it goes against all of our efforts."

Paul: "I see what you mean. Well, I want to apologize."

Stephen: "Thank you. I am also concerned about the quality of your work. It seems like you have taken a dip lately. What has been going on for you lately? It seems that you are on edge."

Paul: "Well, I have been having problems at home."

Stephen: "Anything that you want to talk about?"

Paul: "Not really in detail. It is very personal, but I am not sure my wife and I will be staying together."

Stephen: "I see. Let me know if there is anything I can do to support you. I appreciate you telling me that much. How do you think we should proceed with how you are at work?"

Paul: "Now I am aware that my mood was spilling over and affecting others, I can put up the tin foil."

Stephen: "Put up the tin foil?"

Paul: "Yeah, so others don't get splattered."

Stephen: "Oh. I get it. OK. That sounds good, and now, what about the comments that you made about Nick?"

Paul: "Yes, I know. I will have a talk with him and go over my issues and work something out."

Stephen: "When will you have that done?"

Paul: "By Friday."

Stephen: "OK. Send me a note so that I know it is done and the outcome."

"WE ARE AT A THRESHOLD" REAL CONVERSATION

Margaret, a manager of infomatics, had an even more direct way when things were getting to a critical stage. Kimberly, one of her direct reports, has been not performing well.

> Margaret: "I have noticed a trend in the quality of your work over the last three months. I see an increasing gap between where I think you can perform, and what you are actually accomplishing. I bring this to your attention now because we are at a threshold and things need to change. I have to look at myself first and ask how I can better support you. Kim, I am open to hearing from you in that regard. I'd like to explain to you what I have been noticing in particular, and then have you tell me about your performance and what you think you can do to meet my expectations."

When things get critical, it is useful to put the solution into the other person's hands to actively engage them in solving the problem.

"Without hard work, nothing grows but weeds."
— Gordon B. Hinckley

REAL CONVERSATIONS WITH YOUR PEERS

REAL CONVERSATION, PEER TO PEER, WITH POSITIVE INTENT

Charlie and Art were having a discussion in a peer review meeting.

Charlie: "I think you do really incredible work and the clients are always singing your praises."

Art: "Thanks for that feedback. It feels good to hear that."

Charlie: "Where do you think you can stretch and grow?"

Art: "I think I can do better in my preparation for meetings by doing the final work a few days ahead rather than the night before. That way I won't feel so pressured."

Charlie: "Where do you think I can stretch?"

Art: "The area that I think you can stretch is in closing contracts with clients. You do good work and then leave, but you are not generating work in the way that I think you can."

Charlie: "How do you mean that?"

Art: "You are very proactive when you have an assignment, but it seems that you are not proactive when it comes to creating new work for yourself or other associates. I am not sure what is missing for you, but I expect that a top-rate associate like yourself would be generating more work for the company."

Charlie: "I need to think on that."

Art: "Good. Let me know what you come up with and we can work on some strategies that will move you forward."

In this example, peers set a positive expectation for each other and put themselves into partnership in a win-win situation.

REAL CONVERSATIONS WITH PEERS FROM NEGATIVE TO POSITIVE INTENT

In several instances Shelia had gone to Dorothy, Tom's boss, to handle some difficulties she was having on a cross-functional project that overlapped Tom's area. Tom was not kept in the loop and felt that Shelia was doing an end-around to avoid dealing with him. His frustration and negative intentions came through in his communication.

> Tom: "Shelia, these end-arounds you keep doing to Dorothy are excluding me. Are you trying to make me look bad in Dorothy's eyes? That has got to stop."

> Shelia: "What is your problem? You have no right to take a shot at me." With that, she turned and walked away from Tom.

You can see that these two are in the Drama Triangle. They are on the attack and more than likely will get defensive. Had Tom taken a few minutes to reflect on Shelia's positive intentions, his communication might have gone like this.

> Tom: "Shelia, lately you have been going directly to Dorothy to discuss issues that have overlap in my area. I am getting frustrated because I don't know what is going on and would like to be in the loop of information that regards my area."

Sheila: "First, let me apologize for not talking with you sooner. Dorothy had asked me to have a series of conversations about all the projects I am working on, including the one in your area. She has been looking at my workload and we have been trying to figure out a way to balance my work better for all the services I provide for your business unit. Because of the nature of our conversations, I did not think to talk with you to let you know why I was meeting with her."

Tom: "Wow, thanks for telling me. I can see that I was way off track."

"Expect problems and eat them for breakfast."
— **A. Monapert**

REAL CONVERSATIONS
WITH YOUR BOSS

A Real Conversation with your boss is one of the most challenging and valuable exchanges you'll have at work. Your relationship is obviously a critical one, and it may feel like the stakes are high. Some folks say that giving feedback or engaging with their boss is like trying to play basketball on a minefield! It feels dicey to say the least. There are times when you know you have to express yourself, but how? You want to speak up, but you worry your entire career could be snuffed out with the wave of his or her hand. You want to talk about compensation, development possibilities, and how you are doing, but you fear you may be seen as a troublemaker who has communication issues. Of course, do not speak out and you will be labeled a wimp who cannot step up.

It is a slippery slope. People spend a lot of time trying to figure their bosses out. They tread on eggshells, dreading the threat of retribution, and often fail to walk through their veil of fear and doubt to open their mouths. Ironically, bosses can operate in a vacuum, unaware of their unintentional, but often alienating, impact. Or your boss might announce warmly, "My door is always open," but does that make you feel safe enough to actually walk in and have a candid Real Conversation?

If you sense that your boss is not reaching out to schedule Real Conversations, be proactive. Ask yourself, "What is stopping me from taking the initiative? Why not set up a meeting?" It's your future, right? As long as you remain passive, you will be a Victim to the circumstances rather than a Catalyst to make things happen.

This chapter walks you through tangible steps that will diminish your fears and doubts about talking with your boss. It teaches you how to strike a balance that will make your insights and needs palatable, even when under pressure. Many leaders believe it is up to their people to create the content for important conversations. When you come to the table with your own initiative, questions, options, and solutions, you have a much greater possibility of actually getting what you want and creating a working relationship at the same time.

OPEN DOOR

Regardless of how many stories and anecdotes your boss has told you about how he or she wants feedback, it's always going to feel like a risk to actually engage. You wish your fear would disappear, but that just will not happen. This is good news. When you accept your fears and doubts and attempt to discover what is causing them, you are on the right track toward building the confidence and courage you need. Remember, your feeling of fear can turn into an ally that will serve you well once you identify it and use it to keep you focused, present, and on track.

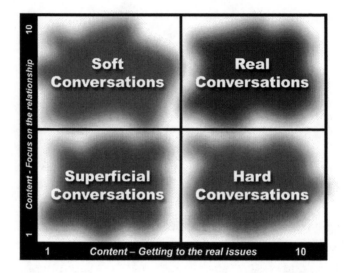

CONTENT AND CONTEXT
REAL CONVERSATIONS

You recall from chapter one the two axis of conversations, Context and Content. These are especially important when talking you're your boss.

Let's look at Context first. It refers to the quality of your working relationship with your boss.

Here's a useful exercise to help you clarify how to build Context for your next Real Conversation with your boss.

Write a list of all of the things that you feel uncertain about when you think of engaging in a conversation with your boss. Most of these sentences can begin with "I don't know _____." Your list might look like this:

I don't know:

- if my boss wants feedback

- when is the best time to give my boss feedback

- how to frame the feedback

- what my boss's hot buttons are

- how to disagree with my boss

- how my boss handles tough feedback

- how to open and end the conversation

As strange as it may seem, this list is actually the agenda for your first Context Real Conversation. Bring your list with you and begin gathering data, answers, and understanding that will frame future conversations. Here's a situation that came up for Brenda that unfortunately had not been preceded by a Context Real Conversation.

Brenda was in a meeting with her boss, Tom, who was presenting the results of Brenda's project to an executive committee. As the presentation unfolded, it was glaringly apparent that Tom was not representing the results accurately. The knot in Brenda's stomach grew as each slide came up and she anxiously wondered if she should interrupt the presentation and provide some corrections. She wanted to at least approach Tom with some feedback after the session, but was afraid to because of past attempts that never went anywhere. She felt stuck.

Brenda never really thought of asking Tom, "What is the best way to give you feedback?" That is because Brenda had never made her list of the Boss's Unknowns and so had never considered having a Real Conversation that was Context-based prior to finding herself in a pretty difficult situation. Had she had that Real Conversation months ago, she would have known exactly how to approach him when something dicey came up for her.

If Brenda had prepared, her earlier Context Real Conversation would have gone something like this.

> Brenda: "You know, Tom, there are times when I may disagree with you, but I don't know quite how to approach you. I'm not sure if you want feedback. If you do, I don't know the best way to give it to you. To be specific, if you are giving a presentation and I have a different opinion of what you are saying, how should I handle that?"

> Tom: "Well, I do want your input. The best way is to do it as soon as possible, as soon as you sense that I've said something or done something. And I'd like you to tell me in private because if it's sensitive information, I certainly don't want it to be in the public domain. I can always go back and correct statements I have made. I have a strong negative reaction when I get feedback in public, so please don't do that."

> Brenda: "Should I just be direct, or is there another way that works?"

Tom: "Sure, direct works, but constructive. Give me specific examples and how you think I should have changed what I said."

Brenda: "While we are on the topic, if I disagree with you, what is the best way for me to disagree with you?"

Tom: "I expect that you would simply say, 'I disagree, and this is why.' I would then expect you to be able to explain why you do not agree with me. That means being able to back your point of view with facts and data. It is very hard for me to be convinced just on a hunch without background information to support it. The bigger the impact of my decision, the more solid I expect your argument to be."

Brenda: "OK, that helps me a lot. Now I know how to effectively approach you."

Tom: "Thanks. Most people don't ask, and I appreciate the effort."

SET THE CONTEXT EARLY

Take time, ideally at the beginning of your relationship with your boss, to have a Context Real Conversation so that you can discover how to give and receive feedback. Clarify their style at a time when you do not have an issue with them and there is no pressure on you. Having this conversation early on sets the table for when a real issue comes up and will build your confidence in approaching them. Many people spend too much time trying to figure out how to give feedback to their boss when a ten-minute Real Conversation would alleviate months of anxiety and worry. Without a clear approach path, you are left with confusion and the need to try to figure out or infer from nonverbal behaviors, innuendos, and other indirect cues and clues how your boss is going to receive your feedback.

Nancy wrote up a one-sheet that had six bullet points; three were the issues and three were the solutions. She gave her list to her boss at the beginning of a Real Conversation and began with, "These are the three things that I want to talk about... These are three solutions that I think could work... Let's talk and see what we can come up with." Having a visual that allows you to have focus points and the clarity to separate the person from the issue is nothing less than brilliant! You both are able to collaborate together, tackle the issues, and build rapport.

Nancy gained the confidence to lead her boss through the conversation. "Do you understand how these are issues for me? Do you see any other issues?" "These are some of the solutions that I thought of regarding the issues. Is there anything else that occurs to you?" A relationship builds and grows on this kind of give and take.

A CASE OF UNCLEAR ROLES AND RESPONSIBILITIES

WHEN ROLES ARE UNCLEAR

M ore often than not, you don't lead by yourself; rather, you do so in partnership with other leaders. This partnership can include peers, your boss or his/her peers, and/or your direct reports. How the two or more of you relate to each other and to the entire staff is very important in that the quality of your relationship has a direct impact on your organization.

In an ideal situation, two such individuals will have complementary skills and perspectives. Tasks and functions can then be divided so that each person can play to their strengths. We will often hear, "I'll deal with the technical side of the business and she'll deal with the administrative side" or "He'll deal with the 'soft' (i.e., 'people') issues and I'll make the scientific decisions." Often these types of "leadership huddles" are informal and to a large degree unintentional in that there are rarely Real Conversations where leaders talk candidly about their strengths and areas for development in a way where they can play to their strengths. It is important that two individuals who are working together to lead a group have Real Conversations about their styles and their strengths and work together to bring out the best in each other.

While some skill sets are tangible and observable, personality traits and communication styles are often less clear. The following true story brings this to light.

Greg, the director, knew most of the staff and placed very high value on the relationships he had with each person. Greg focused to find the positive aspects of each person's contributions but largely ignored situations where people were doing less than expected and rarely if ever gave what he considered to be "negative feedback." He would often say, "You did a very nice job fielding questions in the meeting," while in his mind he had many unspoken criticisms about the quality of the slides the person put together. He missed the opportunity to have a Real Conversation by saying, "You did a nice job fielding questions in the meeting. I have a couple of pointers for you about how you could make your slides better." While Greg's intention was positive he had a blind spot about what was being left out of his conversations with his staff and the resulting impact.

Without realizing it, his avoidance of critical/constructive feedback was resulting in perpetuating sub-optimal work from many of his staff. His avoidance cost him personally as well. He often spent nights and weekends reworking the reports of the junior staff because their managers (Greg's direct reports) were not providing constructive feedback and holding them accountable. Greg didn't realize that his "focus on the positives to the exclusion of constructive feedback" had created poor performance throughout the organization. Because Greg placed such a high value on being positive in the relationship, he tolerated poor quality work. He would often try to give critical feedback, but his desire to not offend anyone caused him to fall short of giving specific clear feedback. As you might guess, the more he tolerated poor quality work, the more the staff turned in poor quality work. And the more they turned in poor quality work, the more frustrated with them he became. Greg's blind spot was that he thought that he could have Real Conversations in which he could be positive, supportive, and constructive at the same time.

Greg was thrilled when he finally hired an assistant director, Sam. Greg was looking forward to having someone to share many of the day-to-day responsibilities. They got a long well and jumped right in to working together without much conversation about how they would be working together and their roles.

Sam came into his role, and like Greg, was a good listener and valued people. He also placed a high value on effectiveness and open communication. When someone was falling short or not being effective in their role, he thought it was important to provide candid and immediate feedback.

On one occasion, a few people came to Sam to complain about their manager. They felt that they were being treated unfairly and were not getting the guidance or support they needed from their manager, Tony. Sam's approach was to meet with this manager and share the feedback. He started the conversation by asking the manager, "How are things going? A couple of your folks approached me the other day with some concerns they did not feel comfortable approaching you directly with. I thought it would be useful for us to have a preliminary conversation and then together decide what the next steps would be."

Sam's aim was to be diplomatic and direct. Prior to this, Tony had never received direct feedback from Greg. He was very upset by the conversation and got defensive. When Sam was discussing the conversation with Greg, Greg reported that he had attempted to provide similar feedback, but was so indirect that his message did not have any impact. Tony was not clear about what was expected nor about what he was doing that was problematic. Although Greg saw what was going wrong, his desire to be positive circumvented telling Tony directly. Later, Tony went to Greg to complain about Sam's message and Greg once again "softened" the message. Even though Greg had the same perception of Tony that Sam did, his softening of the message undermined Sam's leadership effectiveness inside of the organization and perpetuated the poor performance of Tony.

Over time, Sam repeatedly heard examples of how Greg was "too easy" on people, not giving them direct feedback and not holding them accountable for doing quality work. Greg kept people in roles beyond the time they were needed, because they were good people even though their skill set no longer matched the job they were in. Sam found himself surrounded by nice people who thought they were doing a good job but in fact were mediocre performers.

Given Sam's core values and focus on effectiveness, quality work, and direct communication, he began to offer more and more direct feedback. Soon Greg began to hear echoes in the hallway about Sam being "too hard" on people. People came to Greg complaining about Sam and Greg would quickly smooth things over to try to make people feel good. In response, Sam would see Greg being "too easy" on people and became more and more direct with people. Sam thought he was doing the right thing and thought, "Someone around here has to hold people accountable."

So, the higher Greg's tolerance was for poor performance, the lower Sam's tolerance became — the more Greg was "soft" on people, the more Sam felt the need to be "hard" on people. Both of them had positive intentions, but it didn't take long for the entire department to become polarized.

Many staff members perceived that Greg and Sam weren't working very well together and thus were not being good role models for working collaboratively. Sam thought he was having

Real Conversations with the staff but he did not verbalize to Greg his perceptions that he was being too easy on people and undermining the effectiveness of the organization. Greg did not verbalize his perception that Sam was being too hard on the staff.

Once Greg and Sam were able to see the pattern, they came to realize that they were inadvertently feeding into and exacerbating the other person's response, thus bringing about more of the behavior in the other person that they were critical of. They began to see that the staff, not surprisingly, began to play them off against each other to get what they wanted. Upon this realization they sat down and discussed their perceptions of each other and the situation.

Sam: "I would like to see how we can lead and manage the group consistently. I have a few perceptions that I have not discussed with you and would like to get them on the table so we can get some clarity."

Greg: "Sounds good."

Sam: "One perception that I have is that you are not giving people direct feedback. Then when I give them direct feedback they come to you and you dilute or soften it. Let me give you three examples of where I have seen this and then I would like to hear your perception of the situation so that we can have a common understanding of what is going on." Sam continued, giving Greg the three examples.

Greg: "You are right. I do share the same perceptions of what was going on for those three people but I did not verbalize it in the clear way that you did. I see how I undermined your effectiveness by softening the message. I am also painfully aware that I do not like to give negative messages to people, but you seem to be able to be direct and supportive at the same time. How do you do that?"

Sam: "I think my job is to help people be better at what they do. So when I approach them I keep that in mind and I tell them that before I say anything else. I usually ask them how they think they are doing and where they think they can improve. I then ask them if I can share my perceptions of how they are doing. After I give them the feedback I check to make sure they understand what I told them and have a way forward."

Greg came to realize that holding people accountable was not contrary to really caring about people and that in fact having direct Real Conversations with staff could actually strengthen the relationship rather than put it at risk.

After their conversation Greg began being more direct in giving feedback to people. He was not perfect, but with each week his messages got smoother and more natural. When people came to him to complain about Sam's messages, he would ask them, "Have you discussed this with Sam?" If not, he would tell them to talk directly with Sam. Over the next couple of months the overall performance of the organization began to improve. Sam and Greg experienced being aligned and openly discussed issues in the organization and between them when they arose by having Real Conversations.

RETRIBUTION OR REWARD

When you do not know your boss's style or hot buttons, you might unknowingly set up a reaction that will bite you later. How do you get to the place where you do not have to worry about retribution? Retribution occurs when you have failed to have a Context Real Conversation. You need to be fully present. You need to pay attention to the nonverbal signals your boss is sending, and you need to pay attention to what they mean. Is your boss listening? Has she checked out? Is she getting uneasy or even angry?

During a conversation with his boss, Ben vehemently said, "I disagree." He felt confident about his position, but he failed to notice that after he spoke, his boss clenched his jaw and looked away. Had Ben said, "I just noticed something change and I am wondering what you are thinking." Instead, Ben said nothing and his boss clammed up and silently made up his mind that Ben was a difficult person.

Not addressing nonverbal signals puts you at risk that you will hear about "it" later in your performance review. It is not easy to learn how to use what I call "neutral openers," but it is well worth the effort. First, pay attention to the nonverbal signals, and when you see them, immediately address them. Put what you are seeing into descriptive terms that do not have emotional or judgmental associations.

Nonverbal signal	Negative intent interpretation	Neutral opener
Clench jaw	"You're angry."	"I noticed your reaction and am wondering what you are thinking."
Rolls the eyes	"I said something stupid."	"I could not help but notice your reaction and am wondering what you are thinking."
Looks at watch	"He is bored."	"How are we doing on time?"
Looks out the window	"She is not paying attention."	"Are we hitting the right topics? What do you think about what I have said so far?"

Putting The Issues On The Table

Ben was having a difficult time with his boss and did not exactly know how to get the issue on the table. After he did some preparation, he was ready to talk with his boss.

"Over the past three months, I have noticed a dynamic that is becoming increasingly uncomfortable for me. I don't really know how to get this issue out on the table, but feel that at this point we need to talk about it."

"What is happening?"

"It seems as though you are spending a lot of time talking with my direct reports and lower in the organization. You have that right and I would want for them to feel that you are accessible."

"What is problematic then?"

"I am not sure whether is it intentional or not, but what seems to be happening is that my direct reports and their teams are engaging in work that you initiate in these meetings. So I wanted to check it out with you to see if that is what you are intending."

"I was not aware this was happening."

"My direct reports are somewhat confused because they don't know how to prioritize the work that you are asking them to do. Then when they come to me, I have not heard anything about it from you, so then I end up looking like an idiot."

"Basically, I thought I was just thinking out loud. But I can see that this is not how it was taken."

"I wanted to make you aware. Maybe at the end or beginning of your conversations, let them know explicitly that you were just brainstorming, and that you will take it up with me to develop a work plan."

"That sounds like a good idea."

Tips For The Boss — Invite Your Staff To Give You Feedback

George, a vice president of a sales division, tells his team, "If you need something from me or if I'm creating problems for you, I want you to tell me directly, even if it is a tough issue. It is important beforehand that you think about it carefully and consider possible solutions. Even if you have not come up with a solution that works, I want to know that you have given it some thought. Then we can sit down and have a Real Conversation. If you just want to complain, forget it. I do not need you to dump your troubles in my lap. Take a minute and share anything that comes up, first with the person sitting next to you...Now, let's go around the room and hear what some of the issues are."

George regularly enforced his proactive feedback policy by asking his staff individually, in informal settings, "If I could change one thing to be more effective as a leader, what would that be?"

Setting Guardrails

Charlotte's approach is very direct. Whatever the issue is, she tells her team, "Let's sit down and have a Real Conversation about it. Let's resolve it. Once it's resolved, I don't want to revisit it. That will only irritate me. Once we come up with a solid decision, I want to run with it. Again, I do not want to rehash the whole issue once we've come to a resolution." Her staff knew that they could invest quality time in a discussion, but then it was time to move on. Rarely did they have to circle back, waste time, and revisit an old problem.

CONSIDER THIS:

1.   What are the issues you need to discuss with your boss?

2.   What is your biggest concern/fear about giving feedback to your boss? What do you need to know about your boss to feel comfortable giving them feedback?

How would you go about setting up the context with your boss to have Real Conversations in the future?

"You can never quit. Winners never quit,
and quitters never win."
— Ted Turner

THE LAST WORD

Wherever two or more are gathered, there is the possibility for miscommunication. This means that there is also the opportunity for going beyond misunderstanding and negativity to something that is positive and productive.

Real Conversations won't always go perfectly. You will always have challenges. Take the risk and keep working through the issues and soon you will feel it was all worth it. Each Real Conversation builds on the last one and after a while, it will feel normal to build trust in your work relationships by having two-way conversations in which you are fully present and telling the truth. Then it will be time to pass this book on to one of your colleagues.

> *"It is better to lead from behind and to put others in front, especially when you celebrate victory when nice things occur. You take the front line when there is danger. Then people will appreciate your leadership."*
> — **Nelson Mandela**

ABOUT THE AUTHORS

"Don't worry when you are not recognized,
but strive to be worthy of recognition."
—Abraham Lincoln

Jim Peal, Ph.D.
CEO, Leadership Development Group
www.peal.com

Jim's background includes extensive experience that spans across the Pharmaceutical, Biotech Technology, Manufacturing, and Retail industries. Jim's areas of expertise include the integration and alignment of leaders and teams, team-based strategy development, culture integration in mergers and acquisitions, architecting and managing organizational change, transforming dysfunctional teams into productive teams, resolving conflict, executive coaching, and developing and leading executive impact and presentation skills programs.

Jim's reputation as a powerful natural master communicator who is dynamic, multi-talented, fun, and inspiring is the trademark of his 20+ year career. His degree at Baylor Medical School and his doctoral degree demonstrate his ongoing commitment to education, creativity, and excellence. Jim's tenure includes serving as the executive leader of Sage Seminars and the Resource Training Institute. He has also served in executive positions with his partner organizations since 1997. He has trained thousands of executives and health professionals and worked with hundreds of corporate teams from around the world. Jim has been instrumental in empowering businesses to make quantum increases in their productivity. He expresses the depth of his understanding of human beings and systems in an elegant practical speaking and teaching style that enlightens and promotes long-lasting changes.

Jim is the author of the first edition of Daring to Have Real Conversations in Business. Jim's written works include Check Your Attitude at the Door, The Power of Positive Intention (on Amazon — Kindle version available) Ein-Stellungs-Wechsel!, Die Kraft der positiven Einstellung (German version of Check Your Attitude at the Door) on Amazon and Kindle, Power Tools...The Fast Track to Success, and "Is Your 'Politically Correct' Environment Destroying Innovation?" in Manufacturing Today.

Thom Dennis

Phoenix Obsidian

www.facilitation.co.uk

Thom is an experienced educator, speaker, and consultant who for many years was a Royal Marines officer. He has been running his own business for the last 20 years, coaching senior executives through personal and organizational change and facilitating groups of executives to operate as dynamic teams, working together, planning strategically, and making good and timely decisions. He has designed and run leadership courses for over 30 years.

Thom works with CEOs and similarly accomplished executives, helping them to develop themselves and their businesses; he specializes in planning for culture changes, mergers & acquisitions, and the managing of the subsequent impacts of change. He has a wide range of different approaches from Systemic Constellations to Equine-Guided Transformational Learning and draws from his depth of experience in determining how best to work in any given moment.

Thom has a developed sensitivity to talent, culture, and the dynamics in a team and can quickly identify appropriate ways in which to move a situation forward, ways that are likely to have long-term positive impacts on the system as a whole. His approach is always oriented to the performance of the business and the setting and attainment of its goals, combined with much attention to communication.

Thom works in both English and French, frequently facilitating multinational groups in the UK, mainland Europe, the US, Africa, and the Far East. One seminar he completed in KL recently had 26 nationalities in a group of 35 people.

Apart from running his own company since 1994, Thom has experience as a director and also non-executive Chairman. He holds an MSc in Change Agent Skills and Strategies, is a certified NLP Master Practitioner, and is a member of the International Association of Facilitators. He has also studied and practiced organizational constellations for many years and is now expanding this into the equine-assisted arena. His whole approach to any issue is a systemic one with a pragmatic overlay of business sense. He has a sensibility to systems, group dynamics, and culture, which he is constantly honing, and has a reputation for bringing new and innovative approaches to his clients and fellow OD professionals.

Client needs are key and he himself is coached regularly to ensure that dependency both on his part and that of his clients is avoided as well as shining a light on potential shadow matters before they become an issue.

Thom's blend of experience in one of the world's finest armed services, in industry and the City of London, as a director in several businesses, a trained coach, and also a facilitator all bring a unique synthesis of creativity, insight, learning, performance orientation, support, and challenge to his clients.

Trish Barron, MPH

CEO, Barron and Associates

www.barronexecutivecoaching.com

Trish Barron has been guiding CEOs, leaders, and work teams to reach their full potential in her 20+ years as an organizational consultant. By helping people and their organizations operate more effectively, she gives her clients the edge they need to compete in today's marketplace.

Trish has experience working with local, regional, and global organizations in industries such as Emerging Technology, Bio-Technology, Pharmaceutical, Healthcare, Insurance, Federal and State Governments, Non-profits, and Universities.

Trish's view is that most people operate from a place of positive intention. This drives her to provide development and coaching services based on changing underlying beliefs and patterns of behavior. Her style is a blend of good old-fashioned honesty and gentle understanding.

Trish is passionate about helping people have "real" conversations — with themselves and with each other. Through her coaching, she helps people discover their blind spots and then assists them to bring both courage and compassion to all of their conversations. She consistently helps teams to have real conversations that once seemed impossible.

Trish has a Master's Degree in Public Health (Health Behavior and Health Education) from the University of North

Carolina at Chapel Hill and is certified as a Master Practitioner in Neuro Linguistic Programming. She is a certified Tilt Practitioner. She received her Bachelor's Degree in Sociology and Anthropology from The State University of New York at Fredonia.

Zemo Trevathan

President, Zemo Trevathan & Associates, Inc.
www.zemotrevathan.com

Zemo thrives on breaking the rules. Ever since jump-starting his first company in the early 90s, he has been helping his clients do the same thing — figuring out which rules to follow, which new rules to create, and which rules to break. This has always been one of Zemo's strengths — assisting leaders and their teams to identify the "rules" that have become success limitations and replacing these to generate new beliefs, strategies, and pathways to success.

In two decades of service, Zemo has worked with people around the globe in a variety of industries — Pharmaceuticals, Energy, Financial Services, Consumer Goods, Federal and State Government, and Universities, as well as non-profits and start ups. He is especially energized when working across organizational layers — helping executive teams transform company strategy and culture into practical terms and employee engagement.

A former storyteller, Zemo weaves masterful images and experiences, ensuring that hearts and minds are fully and creatively engaged in the process. And, as a homeschooling father, all his organizational work is grounded in a vital sense of prioritization and balance. He imbues the most serious endeavors with spirit and fun, and at the same time holds a firm, hard edge as he supports people at all levels of organizations to bring their best to the table.

Zemo received his BS in Psychology at the University of Puget Sound and currently resides in North Carolina.

> *"I have never met a man so ignorant*
> *that I couldn't learn something from him."*
> **— Galileo Galilei**